LII

MW01230259

PROGRAMMING

2 BOOK IN 1

" Linux For Beginners + Linux". A beginner's Guide For Interfaces, theory, and practice.

By Kevin Davis

LINUX FOR BEGINNERS

LINUX

Linux For Beginners

A Guide for Linux fundamentals and technical overview with a logical and systematic approach.

Text   **Copyright**   ©

Legal & Disclaimer

The information contained in this book and its contents is not designed to replace or take the place of any form of medical or professional advice; and is not meant to replace the need for independent medical, financial, legal or other professional advice or services, as may be required. The content and information in this book has been provided for educational and entertainment purposes only.

The content and information contained in this book has been compiled from sources deemed reliable, and it is accurate to the best of the Author's knowledge, information and belief. However, the Author cannot guarantee its accuracy and validity and cannot be held liable for any errors and/or omissions. Further, changes are periodically made to this book as and when needed. Where appropriate and/or necessary, you must consult a professional (including but not limited to your doctor, attorney, financial advisor or such other professional advisor) before using any of the suggested remedies, techniques, or information in this book.

Upon using the contents and information contained in this book, you agree to hold harmless the Author from

11

and against any damages, costs, and expenses, including any legal fees potentially resulting from the application of any of the information provided by this book. This disclaimer applies to any loss, damages or injury caused by the use and application, whether directly or indirectly, of any advice or information presented, whether for breach of contract, tort, negligence, personal injury, criminal intent, or under any other cause of action.

You agree to accept all risks of using the information presented inside this book.

You agree that by continuing to read this book, where appropriate and/or necessary, you shall consult a professional (including but not limited to your doctor, attorney, or financial advisor or such other advisor as needed) before using any of the suggested remedies, techniques, or information in this book.

Introduction

While not as popular as Windows—at least, for some—Linux is definitely one of the most reliable Operating Systems around—and the best part about it is that it's free, so you don't really have to pay for anything just to get it, and you also wouldn't have to go for counterfeit types of Operating Systems just because you could not pay for the legal copy.

Today, Linux is partly responsible for helping the world work like it should. From people who only work with computers at home, to larger feats such as NASA using Linux-powered computers, it is no surprise why Linux is getting the attention of many—and today; you have the chance to learn about it, and more!

Linux is an operating system. An operating system is software that helps manage all the hardware resources that your desktop computer or laptop is using. Its primary purpose is to handle the communication between your computer software and hardware. If you do not have an operating system, your computer software will not function at all.

Linux is one of the most reliable, stress-free and secure operating systems that we have in the world. It has been here since mid-90s. Over time, it has slowly dominated the market; and today, it is the widely used operating systems on the phones, computers and all other devices that we use these days.

Linux was created initially as a free operating system for Intel x86-based personal computers but as the time went by, it was ported to many other kinds of computer hardware platforms as seen today. It can now be used in so many other computer hardware platforms, much more than any other operating systems out there. It is now the leading system on servers and other major systems like mainframe computers and supercomputers.

This operating system is not the same as it was when it first came into the market. It has been modified and advanced over time in order to suit the different needs of different users. This has worked well because practically anyone can use Linux today.

Linux distributions have come into being over time, and they represent what different users need in an operating system. If you are to install Linux, you will have to choose the kind of distribution that best suits you.

Linux today is being run on embedded systems like mobile phones, tablet computers, televisions, network routers, video game consoles, Android and all other kinds of devices that are in use these days. If you have not been using this as your operating system, you are missing out so much.

Linux is liked for its stability, ease of use, dependability and low cost, among other benefits. So many users have already realized that it is a viable alternative to Windows and all the other operating systems that are already in use.

This book assumes that you are familiar with computers enough to want to explore using Linux. The Linux operating system (OS) is not something your average consumer realizes the extent to which it is the most utilized platform and is tailored to devices such as Android phones, Smart watches, refrigerators, washing machines, video game consoles and DVRs just to name a few.

Linux can be used to host a website, create a new and secure file or e-mail server, diagnose another system you own, and possibly recover crashed files. It can enhance Chromebooks. Even NASA, Dell, IBM, and Hewlett-Packard have tapped into the Linux OS.

It was first developed as a family extension of the various iterations of UNIX. It is free, open-source code and released October of 1991 by Linus Torvalds. Torvalds is a Finnish-American Engineer who believes that open source is the only way to go. Thankfully he thought so. At first, Linux was primarily for personal computers but as you can see it has a use that has expanded exponentially and now runs some of the largest super computers as well as the devices just named.

Since Linux release, other programmers have developed their own versions or distributions of Linux. These are also called **distros**. These next generation developers were able to do this because of the open sourcing of Linux. This is a good thing, but having many different versions has its challenges as you will see.

Technically speaking, Linux is not an operating system per se, as are the distros that are based on the Linux kernel. Linux supported by the larger, Free/Libre/Open Source Software community, a.k.a. FLOSS. This is also sometimes referred to as just Free Open Source Software, or FOSS. Linux kernel version 4.0 was released in 2015. The coding has increased in length exponentially since its development.

Tux is the penguin mascot of Linux. You will see him in his many versions. Some distros flash Tux in different garb or graphic styles. The most popular version of his creation says that he was first named after Linux creator, Linus Torvalds, (i.e., "**T**orvalds **U**ni**X**)", as an entry for a logo contest, which he did not win. Tux does quite well as a mascot, however and everyone who knows Linux associates Tux with great work.

Basic Components of Linux

The **Kernel** is the core, the lowest level of Linux that has control over everything in the system. It talks with the computer's hardware.

The **Shell** (or "sh") is the user interface, the primary way to interact with servers. It provides the directives that are typed through Commands on the Command Line (or terminal) and relays them to the kernel to process between hardware and applications. (To note, Most Linux versions use a shell called Bash, which is "Bourne-Again Shell," although you can use a different shell, but that is probably not for beginners).

The below diagram offers a simple view of how these layers of the Operating System work together.

Linux Graphic by Michael Eagan (2003). Talk for NBLUG, North Bay Linux Users' Group (**http://mike.passwall.com/nblug/kernel-talk**).

Why Choose Linux?

What makes Linux different from other operating systems, and why should you choose it? There are some differences which you should be familiar with if you chose to use Linux over other operating systems.

The things you can do with Linux are virtually endless. Jack of all trades. Some of the most common reasons for a beginner to use Linux include the following.

It is FREE. Free, as in it is Open Source, meaning that the code is open for anyone to use, replicate or change as they see fit. It also is free as in it does not cost money, however that is secondary. The other benefit is that the OS system, in all of its various distributions, are constantly being updated, added to, changed, or inspiring spin offs (the distributions, or distros as you will see), from Linux. Those distributions are also obligated to be open source based on anti-trust laws and licensing that requires any future "family members" to adhere to the same public sharing structure. Nothing is kept secret. Everything is open.

Due to this open sourcing there are communities that center around the development, use and feedback of the various Linux distros. These are advantageous to those newbies who need to know how to do something, how to troubleshoot, or just know how something works. Information exchanges are encouraged. There are many forums online where one can find this type of help, outside of looking at Commands and help pages in the operating system itself.

Another consideration of Linux fans is that you are not dealing with third party companies who may then own or use your data in some way. It is your data, in your storage and sometimes on your server.

One writer described the system as being advantageous to the developing world, in that its source code is offered to resource scarce populations. The possibility for learning technology is supported as well as the source codes can be examined and tinkered with.

Linux is alive. You can use and revitalize older systems. Linux can be installed on old systems. The best part is that you can create what you want or need, and leave the rest behind. You cannot do this with a Windows OS, for example. It is super flexible. You can choose from many environments (for the appearance).

Linux also takes up very little space. As you will see in this guide, you will have an option to run your software entirely off of the hard drive, or even in a virtual environment. You can partition the system and share it with another that you don't want to part with (at all, or at least not quite now).

The applications and programs are on par with offerings of other operating systems such as Windows and MAC OS x. They are not lacking. In fact, something that is available with the Linux Ubuntu distribution is an mp3 player which out does Apple's iPod, since the user runs into many restrictions in their use and portability. Ubuntu's mp3 is freeing.

It is versatile. Depending on which version you choose, you can create a server for e-mail, website, or files. Again, this is a platform for media centers, kitchen appliances, DVR and Wii's, Raspberry Pi's, and international supercomputers. I think you get the point.

It runs other devices. Not only is it interesting to know how things work, but it is a sign of the technological future to come. Get it now.

It is Easy. With a few commands and navigation skills, you can turn your computer into a server or amp up your desktop with ease and speed.

It can be very secure, especially with the server edition which is ultra-secure. Virus software is rarely needed. That is unimaginable for anyone running another Operating System to fathom, but it is true. All of the software and executables are also coming from repositories that are part of the operating system. You won't get that with other systems. These items are digitally signed so you know they are valid and you know where they came from.

You should also know that for as many benefits it has, and although it does have many strengths over other systems in comparison, Linux is not perfect. It is evolving and growing however, so have faith in knowing that glitches particularly in some of the distros are being addressed by developers of these various versions.

Some criticism has to do with glitches in certain distros, limited support, with questions of sustainability of that support, sometimes being oriented to enterprises over personal computers, mobile usage, and other things of that nature.

There are some issues with incompatibility with certain existing computer components (which usually can be patched or repaired). One example is a reported issue with wireless cards. If this happens, depending on the issue, you can do a little research and it is rectifiable in almost all cases.

As some users find that the reasons listed above appear to be "pro" Linux, other users can turn them into "cons". One example is the customization. There are some users that just like the prepackaged features that come along with buying a Windows system, or a MAC system. You won't have to worry about most features and programs having to be located and found. There are many rights there to start with.

Some users fear the use of the CLI, and having to interact via a Command list that can be pages long, and scripts and arguments that can be ten times as long as the base Commands. It can be very intimidating.

Nevertheless, people overwhelmingly like it and find it useful for more than just a home computer operating system as you sees. It has so much in terms of a track record, and so much future potential. Who knows how far it goes, or what innovations it will turn up in next. On that selling point, let it be said that you really should test run Linux. Try it out. Get the experience. You don't have to stay with It, but from we what we know, many people do.

Chapter 1 : Introduction to linux

Originally, Linux was developed merely as a hobby project by a programmer known as Linus Torvalds in the early 1990s while at the University Of Helsinki In Finland. The project was inspired by a small UNIX (an operating system) system called Minix that had been developed by Professor Andy Tanebaum who used the

UNIX code to teach students of that university about operating systems. At that time, UNIX was only used in universities for academic purposes. The professor developed Minix (a little clone of UNIX) to effectively teach his students about operating systems with a bit more depth.

Linus was inspired by Minix and developed his own clone, which he named Linux.

On 5th October 1991, version 0.02- which was the first version of Linux was announced by Linus. While this version was able to run the Bourne shell (bash)- the command line interface- and a compiler called GCC, there wasn't so much else to it.

The version 0.03 was released some time later and then the version number was bumped up to 0.10, as more people began embracing the software. After a couple more revisions, Linus released version 0.95 in March 1992 as a way of reflecting his expectation that the system was prepared for an 'official' release real soon.

About one year and a half later (December 1993), the version was finally made it to 1.0.

Today, Linux is a total clone of UNIX and has since been able to reach a user base spanning industries and continents. The people who understand it see and appreciate its use in virtually everything- from cars to smartphones, home appliances like fridges and supercomputers, this operating system is everywhere. Linux actually runs the largest part of the internet, the computers making all the scientific breakthroughs you're hearing about every other day and the world's stock exchanges.

As you appreciate its existence, don't forget that this operating system was (and still is) the most secure, reliable and hassle-free operating system available before it became the best platform to run servers, desktops and embedded systems all over the globe.

With that short history, I believe you are now ready for some information to get you up to speed on this marvelous platform.

Understanding Linux

Linux is an operating system, just like MAC OS X, Windows 8 and Windows 10. It is software that manages all of the hardware resources related to the desktop or laptop. Do you know what exactly Linux does? In simple words, it is the operating system that is the bridge between your system software and the hardware. The operating system plays a very important part in keeping the unit working and your software functioning.

Why Linux? How is it Different from Other Operating Systems?

Applications ranging from simple office suites to complex multimedia are also featured by Linux. Linus Torvalds developed Linux in the early 1990s in collaboration with other distinguished programmers of the time around the globe. The functions performed by Linux as an operating system are pretty much similar to that performed by other operations systems like Windows, Macintosh, UNIX and Windows NT. Linux stands out from rest due to its free availability, power, and adaptability. Almost all PC operating were developed within the confines of small PCs, and their functioning was limited to restricted PCs. They have become versatile only recently with the up gradation. Upgrading is constantly needed for these operating systems due to the ever-changing capabilities of the PC hardware. Linux was developed under different circumstances. It is a PC version of the UNIX operating system. UNIX has been used on mainframes and minicomputers and now used by network servers and workstations. Linux has brought the speed, flexibility, efficiency and measurability of UNIX to your PC through maximum use of PCs capabilities.

Linux provides GUIs, along with GNOME and KDE, with the same flexibility and power. With Windows and Mac, you don't get the freedom to choose your interface. Linux not only lets you have that freedom, but you can further customize the interface. You can add panels, applications, desktops and menus. You get all the Internet-aware tools and drag and drop capabilities along with these additions.

Historical Context

UNIX operating system was developed in a special context and to completely understand and appreciate Linux, you should understand the basics of UNIX operating system. UNIX was developed in an academic and research environment, unlike other operating systems. The system mostly used in research laboratories, universities, data centers and enterprises is UNIX. The computer and communication revolution has paralleled with the development of UNIX over the past decades. New computer technologies were developed by computer professionals on UNIX, like the ones made for the Internet. The UNIX system is no doubt sophisticated, but it is made to be flexible right from the beginning. Different versions can be made for UNIX after slight or substantial modifications. It is interesting to note that many different vendors have different versions of official UNIX. IBM, Hewlett-Packard and Sun are some examples which sell and maintain their own versions of UNIX. The peculiarity and special needs of a particular research program require UNIX to be tweaked and tailored in conformity with those demands. The flexibility of UNIX doesn't affect the quality, in any way whatsoever. On the contrary, it proves the adaptability of the system which can be molded according to the situation and needs. So Linux was developed in this context with the great adaptability of its predecessor (if we may call it that). Linux is, in fact, a special version of UNIX made for PC. Linux is developed in the same way UNIX was designed, by the computer professional rendering their service in research like environment. Linux is free and publicly licensed. This shows the deep sense of public service and support which UNIX has as it was developed in academic institutions. Linus is accessible to everyone (free of cost), and it is a top rated operating system with its popularity only destined to increase in coming times.

How Linux operates?

Linux is basically divided into three main components: the kernel, the environment, and file structure. The kernel is the main program, controlling and managing the hardware devices like the printer. The environment gives the user with the interface. Commands are received by the environment and transmitted as instructions to the kernel for execution. The way files are stored on the storage system is organized by the file structure. Files are saved and organized in the form of directories. A directory may hold subdirectories, each containing many files. The basic structure of Linux operating system is formed by these three constituents. You can operate the system by interacting and managing files. We will have a look at them separately to form an understanding of how they work.

The operating system has many parts that make it function successfully, and the list of important ones is mentioned below:

The Kernel

It is known to be one of the most important parts of the operating system. No operating system can function properly without this piece. It is the core of the operating system and controls the entire Central Processing Unit. This part has control over the processes occurring in the OS. It is known to be the first element that the system is loaded with, without this, you cannot move forward to the next step. Microkernels were initially used, and they encompassed only the CPU, memory, and IPC. Linux, on the other hand, is a monolithic kernel. It also encompasses the device drivers, file system management, and server system calls. Monolithic kernels are more accessible to hardware and good at multitasking because it can directly access information from the memory or other processes and doesn't have to wait. The Kernel manages the remainder of the system. This part is also responsible for running memory as well as communicating with peripherals such as speakers and others.

The Bootloader

As the name indicates, it is the software that controls the boot procedures of the laptop or computer. Many users would have noticed this as a splash screen popping up and then going away to the boot in an operating system.

With Linux, you get the ability to shift between different versions of Linux kernel or other operating systems you might have installed on your system. A boot management utility, the Grand Unified Bootloader (GRUB) is responsible for selecting and starting a particular operating system or kernel. It is a versatile management tool which not only lets you load different operating systems but also gives you the choice to choose from different kernels installed, and all of this on a single Linux system.

The Environment

The kernel and user interact through an interface provided by an environment. This interface acts as an interpreter. Commands which are entered by the users are interpreted by the interface and sent to the kernel. There are different kinds of environments, namely, desktop, window managers, and command line shells. A user can set his or her user interface. The environments can be altered by the users according to their special needs, regardless of the kind of environment they opt. The operating system works as an operating environment for the user, in this respect which can be controlled by the user. It is known to be among one of the most creative and interesting programs. It is a puzzle that the users interact with. This program is also one of the most interactive pieces of the operating system. The system has a number of desktop environments to select from according to their preferences, such as Cinnamon, KDE, Enlightenment, XFCE, Unity, etc. Every desktop environment has a number of built-in applications like web browsers, games, tools, configurations and more.

The environment plays a vital part in the working of Linux. We will have a look at two most popular environments in order to understand what they entail.

GNOME

GNOME also known as GNU Network Object Model Environment is powerful and most popular Linux desktop environment. It can be easily managed by the user, and especially if you are a beginner. It consists primarily of a desktop, a panel, and a set of graphical interface tools with the help of program interfaces are usually constructed. GNOME is designed in such a way that it can provide a flexible platform for the development of exciting and powerful applications. Almost every distribution support GNOME while Red Hat and Fedora serve it as their primary interface. GNU Public License deals with its release, and it is free of cost. The source code, documentations, and other GNOME software can be easily downloaded from their website at gnome.org

Most Ubuntu distribution users are familiar with GNOME. The reason for its popular lies in the fact that it is easy to use, and also because it is fairly low on the system resources. As a beginner, you will love GNOME, but it doesn't mean that advanced users dislike it. The environment can be configured according to your likings as it has quite a few advanced settings available. It's fairly unique, and it will not be fair to compare it with the latest desktop environments. If you are counting on appearance, it resembles more like Mac than Windows, and it is because the menu bar resides at the top whereas the task bar is at the bottom of the interface (especially in Ubuntu's new Unity interface).

KDE

K Desktop Environment (KDE) includes all the standard desktop features like file manager and window manager. It is a network-transparent desktop that has an exclusive set of applications that can do almost all Linux tasks. It is completely integrated with the internet as it is an internet aware system. Internet applications like Mailer, newsreader, and internet browser are available in KDE. The file manager also works as the Web and allows you to browse the internet directly. KDE serves a dual purpose; where it provides the ease of use for Windows and Macintosh, it brings the flexibility of the Linux operating system.

KDE is a bit heavier on the system resources, and also it is a bit more complex than GNOME. Instead of aiming to create an easy to use interface, KDE developers are always looking to evolve, and add more functionality to their prior KDE versions, affecting the beginners with these kinds of versions. However, its interface is very attractive, and it has an exciting desktop comprising of widgets. If you are counting on appearance, it resembles more like Windows, the task bar, and the main menu are located at the bottom of the interface. The main menu resides at the bottom left, and can be used if you want to launch applications or view settings. The complexity of KDE can be understood with the help of the following problems. Firstly, it is very difficult to figure out where the settings you want to change are located. It is because there are various setting options and preference panes, which are pretty much confusing. Even if you are comfortable using Linux, or say computers, as a whole, you will still find it difficult to navigate. KDE offers various configuration options that are available in the main menu, but the problem arises that you cannot find the proper setting. Secondly, it also has some characteristics that can be confusing, especially for the beginners and new users. If you are dragging and dropping files anywhere, it always asks the user whether to move or copy that particular file, and it is that kind of problem which you can't seem to change. KDE is a great choice for the advanced users, who are looking for a lot of configuration options, but there is always room for learning, and KDE will try to challenge their knowledge time to time.

Getting Started

Using Linux is quite easy as it provides a user friendly interface, which includes the graphical logins and GUIs (graphical user interfaces) like KDE and GNOME. It was difficult for the general public to interact with the command line interface but now even the standard Linux command line has become more users friendly. The commands can be edited, history list can be viewed, and the introduction of cursor-based tools has revolutionized the Linux system, as a whole.

There are two basic requirements of using Linux. The first requirement is that you should know how to access your Linux system, and secondly, you should know how to execute commands so that you can run the applications. Access can either be granted through the command line login or the default graphical desktop login. For the graphical login, a simple window pops up comprising of menus and options. The username and password can be fed in the appropriate fields to gain access. Once you gain access through the graphical login, you can interact with either the command line or a GUI. Interacting with GUI is quite easy as it comprises of the interface just like Windows.

The Shell

Shell is a type of an environment, but it can be considered as a separate entity. It interprets commands through a line-oriented interactive and non-interactive interface between the operating system and the user. The commands are entered on a command line, which is then interpreted by the shell and sent to the operating system as instructions. The commands can also be placed as script files which can be interpreted collectively. The shell is a program that controls the user's interaction. It is a process that allows the user to take complete control over the computer through the commands they type in the text interface. It is not a part of the kernel but uses it to create files, perform programs and much more. In simple words, it is the program that takes all the commands from the keyboard to the operating system.

Many different types of shells have been developed for Linux. Bourne Again shell (BASH), Korn shell, TCSH shell, and the Z shell are some of the prominent ones. A user only needs one type of shell to get the work done. BASH shell is set as default so you will be using this shell unless you specify or opt another.

Daemons

It is a program that runs as a background procedure. This program is not under the direct control of the user. Daemons controls the background services such as sound, printing, etc. that start during the boot or after you have logged into the desktop. The processes under this program end with the letter D. this clarifies that the procedure is a Daemon.

Applications

Where applications are concerned, the desktop environment does not offer the users with a number of options. Linux provides the users with millions of superior quality software titles, just like the MAC and Windows that can be installed. The modern distributions that are included in Linux include tools that are similar to the App-store. These applications centralize and also make the installation procedure simple for you. For example, Ubuntu Software Center has millions of applications that you just have to install and not pay anything for.

Graphical Server

It is the system that holds half of the responsibility to display graphics on the screen. The Graphical Server is usually referred as X or the X server. It is made to act flexibly, and you can configure it in many ways. It works on all the window cards that are available. It is not limited to a specific desktop interface. It provides a range of graphical operations that file managers, window managers, and even desktops can use, among other user interface applications.

The Distribution

The Distribution is known to be the highest layer of the operating system. It is the program that contains all the layers as mentioned above. As the kernel is the first thing to get installed in the operating system, the distribution is the last. Without it, the system does not get completed. The makers of the Distribution layer decide which system tools, applications, kernel, and environment should be included to be used by the users.

There are several distributions of Linux although; there is one standard version of Linux. Different groups and companies have packaged Linux in a slightly different manner. The company releases the Linux package usually in the form of CD-ROM. They can later release the updated versions or new software. The kernel which is centrally used by all the distributions is acquired through kernel.org. Although the kernel used is the same, it can be configured differently by the distributers.

It is not very complicated to install the Distribution. It can be done with the help of a CD that contains the particular software for installation as well as configuration. The commercial companies or a professional individual either maintains this layer. For the convenience of the users, the best distributions offer them with a great application management system. This system will allow the users to find, and then install, the applications they want with just a few clicks of the mouse. This is the layer that makes searching simple, and applications installation is just a few clicks away. Linux has 350 distributions available for the users. Listed below are the popular Linux distributions:

Deepin

Fedora

Linux Mint

Ubuntu Linux

Debian

Arch Linux

OpenSUSE

Every distribution will have a dissimilar feeling and look on the monitor. A few have a contemporary user interface such as Deepin, Ubuntu, etc. On the other hand, others have a traditional environment such as OpenSUSE.

When you have Linux, you get all the choices. With the choices, also comes confusion. With many options available for Linux Desktop, which one is the most appropriate for you? Which desktop is the most user-friendly? There are no compulsory rules or tests that you need to follow to choose your desktop destination. It is all about your likes and features. When you look at the desktop functionality in detail, you will notice that there is certainly a connection between the desktop and the user. Mentioned below are the details of a few Linux desktops:

Ubuntu

Do you want a modern interface connecting to the local data as well as hundreds of remote sources? Users who wish to stay connected to social media want quick access to shopping websites, etc. will find Ubuntu as the best option. The users who would want to spend maximum time on the keyboard will prefer the Ubuntu Utility desktop. This form is certainly very efficient in interacting with the users. Ubuntu is the best choice for the users who want everything at their fingertips without caring a lot about the feel as well as the look of the desktop.

GNOME 3

For the users who want a contemporary desktop with keeping the look and feel fresh, can choose GNOME 3. It has a minimalistic approach to an extensive desktop. On the desktop, you will not find many items which give you a feeling of minimal interaction. But when you open the dash, you will find plenty of interactive items. The Ubuntu locks some of the interfaces while this option allows tinkering. In case you are looking for a modern feel just like Ubuntu, but with some more tinkers, then GNOME 3 is made for you.

KDE Project

KDE Project is the distribution for KDE. A complete and developed desktop environment for the Linux operating system is KDE. This environment has had a few major changes that were required to be made for functionality. Thus, whatever the environment does, it does it brilliantly. It is the environment that has nothing else but the start menu, system tray, and panel. Since this environment has a modern touch, it still has some hold from the Windows generation, XP/7 to be precise. This option is perfect for those people who do not prefer change. Users who want the Windows design will prefer this environment because it is similar to Windows, but with a more modern look and simple transitions.

Enlightenment

It is an altogether different environment when compared to the others. While you initiate this environment, you start to notice the change. It is very different, as it does not have the start panel and menu, but a desktop menu and unique elements. However, this environment of the Linux OS is certainly not made for everyone. Those who want a unique, and ready to use simple environment can choose Enlightenment. Obviously, all of the uniqueness comes with a price tag.

This desktop environment wants you to learn about it before you install so that it is not very tough for you to get a handle on it. Those who love to tinker with unique things will love this Linux desktop environment. Enlightenment comes with plenty of themes. The themes do not only have a changed desktop color but also a few changed details. It is perfect for the user who loves change and wants a change on the desktop screen often.

Deepin

The latest entry to the Linux operating system environments is Deepin. Just after the entry, this landscape has managed to attract a lot of people. It gives an amazingly modern look and feel to the desktop. The main thing about this landscape is that it combines all of the great desktops into one. It has a very attractive and unique control panel. The users will love exploring the new landscape. They will be pleased to find amazing features with a modern approach. Those looking out for a unique and simple landscape can have the best experience using this.

Essential Parts Of A Linux System

Just like other Mac OS X and Windows 10, Linux is an operating system. It is made up of the following pieces:

The bootloader- This is the software that manages your computer's boot processes. Simply put, it is the splash screen that pops up and then disappears to boot into the operating system.

The kernel- If you've done some research into Linux before, you should have come across this word countless times. It refers to the piece of the whole that's referred to as **Linux**. It is the core of the system; it manages peripheral devices, CPU and memory.

Daemons- These are the background services such as scheduling, sound and printing that either starts when you log into your computer or during the boot process.

Shell- You've probably also heard this word too many times as well or the **Linux command line,** which at one time scared many people away from Linux (perhaps because they thought they had to learn some mind-numbing command line structure to use the OS). The shell is the command process that lets you control your computer through commands by typing them into a text interface. Today, you can work with Linux without even touching the command line but it's important to work with it, as we are going to see shortly.

Graphical server- This is simply the sub-system that displays graphics on your monitor. It is commonly known as x or the x server.

The desktop environment- This is the actual implementation of the metaphor 'desktop' that is made of programs running on the visible surface of the operating system that you will interact with directly. You have numerous desktop environments to choose from which include gnome, enlightenment, xfce, utility and cinnamon. The desktop environment comes with a bundle of built-in applications, which include configuration tools, file managers, games and web browsers- among others.

Applications- As you may already know, desktop environments don't usually offer the full array of apps. Linux provides thousands of software titles, which you can easily access and install, which is the same case with Windows and Mac.

The above descriptions will assist you sail through the rest of the book easily. Let's now get to the part where we start using the program. The first step is choosing the distribution, as you will find out next.

Choosing Your Distribution (Distro)

Before we get started with the command line, we have to make sure you are all set up. The first thing you need to do therefore is select your distribution. Unlike Windows, Linux doesn't have a single version, and that's why we have many Linux 'distributions'.

These distributions take the kernel and combine it with other software such as a desktop environment, graphical server, web browser and many more. A distribution thus unites all these elements into one operating system that you can install and work with.

From a beginner user versions to intermediate and advanced user versions, there are versions to suit any level or need. All you have to do is download your preferred version into a USB thumb drive and install it to any number of machines you like.

Which distribution should you go for?

You need a distro that is easy to install, it needs to have great applications on it and needs to be easy to use for everyday activities. Moreover, the distro needs to be easy to tweak when the need arises. It is for these reasons that I recommend the tiny core distro that weighs about 11 MB.

Introducing... tiny core!

Besides satisfying those parameters, tiny core saves so much on size and only requires you to have a wired network connection during its initial setup. The recommended amount of RAM you need here is only 128MB.

Well, you can take other considerations while choosing your distro, but it all depends on what you want to use it for. The distro we'll work with here is clearly ideal for someone who's just dipping their feet into Linux-without any considerable experience.

Also known as TCL, Tiny core Linux is a very specific distro, specially designed to be nomadic. Just like other distros, you can bring it with you and run it from a USB drive, CD or hard disk.

For this section, we're going to be using TCL as an example of how you can download and install a Linux distro.

Myths About Linux

Despite its proven benefits over other operating systems, many people are very reluctant to switch over to Linux because they have heard multiple myths about it. This chapter will explore some of the myths surrounding Linux and give the true information about it.

Myth #1: Linux is hard to use.

The fact is that all operating systems are different and take some getting used to. If you have ever gone between Windows and Mac OS, you know all about this problem. Navigating the Windows OS is very, very different than figuring things out on Mac. However, you don't just give up and say that it's too hard to learn, especially not if you just invested a lot of money in a new OS! No, you learn how to use it and gradually adjust. After a few weeks or so, it becomes second nature and you don't even have to think about what you are doing.

The same principle applies to Linux. It isn't necessarily harder than Windows, Mac, or any other OS. Rather, it is different. You need to give yourself some time to get used to the interface and how the desktop program works. Give yourself a few weeks, and you will probably find that Linux is actually easier than many other operating systems.

Myth #2: Linux is command-line only.

When Linux was first created, GUI technology was in its infancy. As a result, nearly all operating systems used command-line interface instead of the graphics interface that you have come to know and love. Until the mid-1990s, Microsoft used MS-DOS, which was a command-line interface. This was the period when Linux began its rise to popularity, so many people came to associate it with its command-line interface.

Today's Linux systems use a GUI interface, so you will still get the graphic desktop with icons that you can click on. You can also use Linux exclusively in command line, and some people find that this is the best way to get the most out of Linux. However, for most users, the GUI interface is more than satisfying in meeting their computing needs. You can use Linux without ever having to learn any command line.

Myth #3: Linux lacks the variety of applications that other operating systems have.

It's true that Linux does not have as many applications as are available on Windows and Mac. However, think of how many different applications you can download for, say, writing up your weekly grocery list. Really, you just need one application for that! While Linux has fewer applications (fewer apps that allow you to create that weekly grocery list), it has an amply sufficient variety to meet all of your needs (there still are apps for your weekly grocery list, just not as many).

Also consider that between Mac and Windows, not all applications are compatible with both platforms. You usually have to download one version of an application for Mac and a different version for Windows. There are some applications that simply don't work on Mac or that don't work on Windows. The fact that this principle also applies to Linux should not deter you from using it.

Most major applications, like Skype, are compatible with Linux. You can still use them to get the most out of your Linux experience.

Myth#4: You can't be a gamer with Linux.

True, if you are a die-hard gamer who lives in your mother's basement and plays games instead of working for a living, you may find that Linux isn't strong enough. However, for casual gamers, like those who enjoy playing Fantasy Football on the weekend, there are plenty of Linux distributions that support that lifestyle. Steam, the gaming website, has over 3000 games that are compatible with Linux and even has its own Linux-based gaming console. As an added bonus, if you are a 90s throwback kid, you can use the Linux Terminal to play arcade games!

Ubuntu is a great distribution that you can use if you are a gamer and want to use Linux. The same games may not be as immediately available as they are on Windows, but you should be able to access them quickly enough.

Myth #5: Linux isn't for computer desktops.

Many major companies, including NASA, today use Linux to power their servers. It is also growing quickly in the Internet of Things (the Internet of Things is the connectivity between different appliances, like cars, refrigerators, coffee pots, and home security systems). This has led to the myth that Linux is best-suited for servers, not for the desktops that most people use for their personal and work computing.

The fact is that while Linux is strong enough to help build the Internet of Things and power NASA servers, it is also ubiquitous enough for casual use on people's desktops. You can use it to surf the web, edit pictures, upload files, do your word processing, create spreadsheets, and any other number of things that you usually do on your desktop.

Myth #6: Linux is not secure.

The fact that Linux's source code is publically available to anyone who wants to view it has led to the myth that Linux is not secure. However, this could not be farther from the truth. The next chapter will get into more detail about how Linux is actually more secure than other operating systems because of how it is fundamentally structured and the types of access that users have. For now, understand that while the source code is publically available, this doesn't mean that anyone can go in and infiltrate it with a virus. Changes to the code are moderated and must be approved.

Myth #7: Linux is so unpopular that it isn't worth learning it.

True, most companies and businesses use Windows as their preferred operating system. However, the fact that many government organizations use Linux should clue you in to the fact that it is highly valuable. In fact, people who are trained in Linux, especially in tech support roles, are able to make significantly more money. This is partly because it is a rarer skill, and partly because of the high-profile organizations that use it. Possibly the biggest hindrance to the further growth of Linux lies in the fact that there aren't enough people trained in it.

Myth #8: Linux software is pirated.

This is simply not true. People willingly create the source code that is used for Linux and donate it. The fact is that many commercially-sold softwares, like from Microsoft, are created off of source codes that were designed for public use.

Myth #9: Linux destroys intellectual property.

The fact that Linux is available for free has led to the belief that people aren't able to hold the rights to their own intellectual property; rather, it has to be distributed freely in a type of socialism. While that belief may be understandable based on a superficial understanding of Linux, the truth is quite the opposite. Monopolies, like Microsoft during the 1990s, destroy intellectual property and impede creative development. They often take the ideas that were created by individuals and incorporate them into their own structures, thus depriving the creators of the rights. The fact that Linux is free means that people can willingly distribute their intellectual property, not that they disown it. In fact, when you submit a coding patch and it is accepted, you sign your name on it!

Myth #10: Linux is on its way out.

After all, how sustainable can free, open-sourced software be? People need to get paid for their work. And besides, you get what you pay for. If you download something that is free, it is probably of very poor quality.

Not at all true. The fact that Linux is free means that anyone can use it; it is an exercise of what the creators believe is a basic right of computing: it should be accessible to anyone. The fact that it is open source means that there is a vastly larger pool of contributors who can apply their own creativity and ingenuity to improving it. And as Chapter 7 will explain, the process of getting a coding patch approved is very extensive. There is a high standard of excellence employed by the team at the Linux Foundation.

These are just some of the myths surrounding Linux and the actual truths behind them. If you find that you have additional reservations other than what was explained in this chapter, you are encouraged to get online and do your own research. Uncover the truth for yourself so that you can decide if Linux is right for you.

Accidents can happen anytime without any warning bells. So, it is extremely important to have a safe place to store the data with the use of other hosts, tapes, floppy disks as well as CDs.

A reliable backup tool is something that is certainly not optional, and everyone should have one. This definitely does not imply that you need to spend a whole fortune on the backup to get a setup. A backup expense is one thing that you need to keep ready because you never know when the need will arise.

The administrative duties are not accomplished without backup operations, as they are an integral part of the administrative functions. The traditional dump/restore tools help you refine your backup process, as they detect data changes since the last backup.

Computer software utility, tar, helps in backing up and restoring particular files and directories in the form of archives. For backup purposes, tar is usually utilized with a tape device. The backups can be scheduled automatically by scheduling the suitable tar commands with the cron utility. You can also compress the archives to save the storage space. The compressed archive material can thus be extracted from the system to any medium, such as floppy disk, tape, or a DVD. However, while working on GNOME, you can utilize the option of File Roller to create archive files readily. In contrast, the KDAT tool on KDE back up archives to tapes which are believed as a front end to tar tool.

There are a number of solutions available in the market. A few are cost effective and have minimal features; others are expensive and full of features. There are several backup solutions available for the

Linux operating system, and some popular and effective ones are mentioned below:

- **Bacula**
- **Fwbackups**
- **Mondorescue**
- **Rsync**
- **Amanda**
- **Simple backup solution**
- **Back in time**
- **Box backup**
- **Arkela**
- **Kbackup**
- **Areca backup**
- **Afbackup**
- **Tar**
- **Dump**
- **Cedar backup**
- **Duplicity**
- **Rsnapshot**
- **PING**
- **Partimage**
- **Clonezilla**

- **Zmanda**

- **Timevault**

- **Flyback**

- **AMANDA**

Below are some pointers that you need to know regarding the Linux backup techniques:

- **Create, question and the unpack the file archives**

- **Make Java archives**

- **Encrypt your important data**

- **Write a CD**

- **Look for important data to use the other backup**

When choosing a backup for the Linux operating system, it is important for you to look for things such as auto-changers, backup media, open source software, data format, cross-platform support, volume shadow copy, reports and alerts, commercial support, deduplication, backup span multiple volumes, encryption data stream, etc.

Choosing the Right Backup Tool

The problem of choosing the right backup option is an important one. There are many options available. You should be able to find the one which works best for your needs. To help you choose, we will have a look at some popular backup options along with their pros and cons.

Amanda

The cons would include the centralization of the Amanda backup system. If your backup requirement does not include tapes or media, Amanda is not the right choice as it includes continuous filling up and changing; besides you would have to rely on a central server to manage everything. It is better to opt for a simpler solution as your needs may overkill Amanda. If your work requires media and a central system, you will really find Amanda the best option with its efficient backup and the ability to write tape and disk at the same time.

Bacula

Bacula is considered a good alternative to Amanda, but again it depends on your requirement. Like Amanda, Bacula is an open source and free to use. In order to use Bacula, you have to install client programs on every machine you want the backup for. It is controlled through a central server. Bacula uses its own file format instead of standard Unix tools for backup.

When you're using more than one server with different tape drives, Bacula is a better alternative as it does incremental and full routine backups. Encryption and RAIT are supported by Amanda whereas Bacula has a scripting language for customization. You can seek help from this language to create encryptions.

While deciding which of these two backup systems would work best, it comes down to your requirements and architecture. The preference of your staff should also be taken into consideration. If you're using a central backup server with one tape drive, Amanda will work best for you, and if you're using tape drives that are distributed across the network, Bacula would be the right pick.

BackupPC

BackupPC is designed for backing up Linux or WinXX laptops and desktops to a file server; it is also a free and open source. It is known for its high performance. It is being used at smaller scale operations efficiently.

The features offered include the ability to store and keep snapshots of a small company's desktop for a long period of time. Users can restore their own backups, the presence and absence of a particular computer (roaming laptop) can be detected. Reminders are given automatically in case you haven't backed up in sometime.

The web interface available to the user and the administrator can be used to initiate backups. Every file is stored in a specified and individual archive which allows an ease of access and quick recovery of both single files and a group.

The downsides of using BackupPC is its slow performance while doing large restores. It is also not a viable option for remote use in case you have a lot of data. The archives which you have compressed can only be read by tools of BackupPC which makes you completely reliant. The positive side is that being an open source, you can always keep the source code so that you have continuous access to the program.

Rsync

Different Linux backup solutions have rsync at the back end. It is a good tool which can be used in combination with scripting to make remote mirrors and other backup schemes. People who don't think they need a special backup tool personally or commercially will prefer this method.

Rsync can be run as a server daemo. It will give access to remote users to sync file copies to your system while keeping the entire directories and only transferring the changed files. You can update files without downloading the full version as mirror and software FTP sites which act as rsync servers.

Rsync can be used to remote-copy files or a directory from one host to another, making an intelligent and specific backup. Rsync is designed to copy only those files have been tweaked instead of the whole directory. The archive mode saves the ownership and permissions, giving the relevant users access through the host system.

The simple setup of this tool makes it a good choice while doing an impromptu backup. Rsync works best when you need more backup in the form of duplication (this can include copying the files, directories, and website content to a different site).

Commercial Linux backup products

Symantec Corp.'s Vertias NetBackup Enterprise is a good option if you're looking for commercial Linux backup product. It is an enterprise-level server that provides support for Windows, many Unix flavors, and Linux. It also offers special support to various virtual environments like VMware.

NetBackup maintains a dashboard which provides insight into capacity, the trends, the charges and costs of recovery and backup services, compliance and more. This is the best option for you if you don't want to maintain your own reporting or find other solutions you're using unsatisfactory.

Symantec's Backup Exec along with Linux agent and BakBone Software's NetVault are other popular commercial backup solutions.

Having a solid backup and recovery plan is a must when you're looking for a Linux backup tool. The solution doesn't work until you've tested your ability to restore data. You have to look at it in the bigger picture when choosing the backup software. This will ensure that you're protected, in the real sense.

What are Linux Distributions?

When you get Linux for your computer, you are essentially getting Linux distribution. Just like other popular operating systems, you get an installation program that consists of the kernel, a graphical user interface, a desktop, and a bunch of applications that you can readily use once you installed Linux in your computer. The added bonus is that you also get the opportunity to get your hands on the source code for the kernel and the applications that you get, which allows you to tweak them the way you want them to operate in the future.

There are several available Linux distributions that you can use to date, which you can view at distrowatch.com. In this website, you can read more information about specific distributions and find website links where you can get the installation disk or download files.

While you can add desktop environments, apps, and drivers that don't come with your distribution, you will need to find the distribution that will give you the ideal setup that you have in mind. Doing so will save you the time that you may need to spend on finding apps and other programs that will work best with the Linux that you have installed, which can get in the way of setting up the system just the way you want it.

What Comes with a Distro?

1. GNU software

Most of the tasks that you will be performing using Linux involve GNU software. These are utilities that you can access using the text terminal, or the interface that looks like a Windows command prompt where you enter commands. Some of the GNU software that you will be using are the command interpreter (also known as the bash shell) and the GNOME GUI.

If you are a developer, you will be able to make changes to the kernel or create your own software for Linux using a C++ compiler (this already comes with the GNU software that comes with your Linux distro) and the Gnu C. You will also be using GNU software if you edit codes or textfiles using the emacs or the ed editor.

Here are some of the most popular GNU software packages that you may encounter as you explore Linux utilities:

autoconf	Generates shell scripts that automatically configure source-code packages.
automake	Generates Makefile.in files for use with autoconf.
bash	The default shell (command interpreter) in Linux.
bc	An interactive calculator with arbitrary-precision numbers.
Binutils	A package that includes several utilities for working with binary files: ar, as, gasp, gprof, ld, nm, objcopy, objdump, ranlib, readelf, size, strings, and strip.
Coreutils	A package that combines three individual packages called Fileutils, Shellutils, and Textutils and implements utilities such as chgrp, chmod, chown, cp, dd, df, dir, dircolors, du, install, ln, ls, mkdir, mkfifo, mknod, mv, rm, rmdir, sync, touch, vdir, basename, chroot, date, dirname, echo, env, expr, factor, false, groups, hostname, id, logname, nice, nohup, pathchk, printenv, printf, pwd, seq, sleep, stty, su, tee, test, true, tty, uname, uptime, users, who, whoami, yes, cut, join, nl, split, tail, and wc.
cpio	Copies file archives to and from disk or to another part of the file system.
diff	Compares files, showing line-by-line changes in several different formats.

ed	A line-oriented text editor.
emacs	An extensible, customizable, full-screen text editor and computing environment.
Findutils	A package that includes the find, locate, and xargs utilities.
finger	A utility program designed to enable users on the Internet to get information about one another.
gawk	The GNU Project's implementation of the awk programming language.
gcc	Compilers for C, C++, Objective-C, and other languages.
gdb	Source-level debugger for C, C++, and Fortran.
gdbm	A replacement for the traditional dbm and ndbm database libraries.
gettext	A set of utilities that enables software maintainers to *internationalize* (make the software work with different languages such as English, French, and Spanish) a software package's user messages.
ghostscript	An interpreter for the PostScript and Portable Document Format (PDF) languages.
ghostscript	An interpreter for the PostScript and Portable Document Format (PDF) languages.
ghostview	An X Window System application that makes ghostscript accessible from the GUI, enabling users to view PostScript or PDF files in a window.
The GIMP	The GNU Image Manipulation Program, an Adobe Photoshop-like image-processing program.
indent	Formats C source code by indenting it in one of several different styles.
less	A page-by-page display program similar to more but with additional capabilities.
libpng	A library for image files in the Portable Network Graphics (PNG) format.
m4	An implementation of the traditional Unix macro processor.
make	A utility that determines which files of a large software package need to be recompiled, and issues the commands to recompile them.
ncurses	A package for displaying and updating text on text-only terminals.
patch	A GNU version of Larry Wall's program to take the output of diff and apply those differences to an original file to generate the modified version.
rcs	Revision Control System; used for version control and management of source files in software projects.
sed	A stream-oriented version of the ed text editor.
Sharutils	A package that includes shar (used to make shell archives out of many files) and unshar (to unpack these shell archives).
tar	A tape-archiving program that includes *multivolume support* — the capability to archive *sparse files* (files with big chunks of data that are all zeros), handle compression and decompression, and create remote archives — and other special features for incremental and full backups.
texinfo	A set of utilities that generates printed manuals, plain ASCII text, and online hypertext documentation (called info), and enables users to view and read online info documents.
time	A utility that reports the user, system, and actual time that a process uses.

2. Applications and GUIs

Since you will not want to type string after string of commands on a command terminal just for your computer to do something, youw will want to navigate and use programs in your computer using a GUI or a graphical user intergace. A GUI enables you to click on icons and pull up windows that will help you use a program easier.

Most of the distros use the K Desktop Environment (KDE), or the GNU Object Model Environment (GNOME). If you have both environments installed on your computer, you can choose which desktop will serve as the default, or you can switch between them from time to time. Both these desktops have a similar feel to Mac OS and Windows desktops. It is also worth taking note that GNOME comes with a graphical shell called Nautilus, which makes the Linux configuration, file search, and application loading easier. Should you need to use a command prompt, all you need to do is to click on the terminal window's icon on both desktop environments.

Apart from GUIs, any average computer user will also need to to use applications, or programs that you can use to perform basic computing needs. While you may not have access to the more popular programs that you may have used in a Mac or Windows computer, Linux can provide open-source alternatives that you can try out. For example, instead of having to buy Adobe Photoshop, you can try out The GIMP, which is a program that works just as great when it comes to working with images.

Linux also offers productivity software packages which fulfills the bulk of an ordinary computer user's needs.

You can get office productivity apps that will allow you to do word procesing, create database, or make spreadsheets from Libreoffice.org or OpenOffice.org.

Tip: If you want to install MS applications to Linux (e.g., Microsoft office), you can use CrossOver Office. You can download this app from www.codeweavers.com/products/crossover-linux/download).

3. Networks

Linux allows you to find everything that you need by using a network and exchange information with another computer. Linux allows you to do this by allowing you to use TCP/IP (Transmission Control Protocol/Internet Protocol), which allows you to surf the web and communicate with any server or computer out there.

4. Internet servers

Linux supports Internet services, such as the following:

- Email
- News services
- File transfer utilities
- World wide web
- Remote login

Any Linux distro can offer these services, as long as there is Internet connection, and that the computer is configured to have Internet servers, a special server software that allows a Linux computer to send information to another computer. Here are common servers that you will encounter in Linux:

- in.telnetd – allows you to log in to a different system wia the internet, with the aid of a protocol called TELNET

- sendmail – serves as a mail server which allows exchange of emails between two systems using the Simple Mail Transfer Protocol (SMTP)

- innd – allows you to view news using the Network News Transfer Protocol (NNTP), which enables you to access a news server in a store-and-forward way.

- Apache httpd – allows you to send documents to another system using the HyperText Transfer Protocol (HTTP).

- vsftpd – allows you to send a file to another computer using the filetransfer protocol (FTP)

- sshd – allows you to log-in to a computer securely using the internet, using the Secure Shell (SSH) protocol

5. Software Development

Linux is a developer's operating system, which means that it is an environment that is fit for developing software. Right out of the box, this operating system is rich with tools for software developments, such as libraries of codes for program building and a compiler.

If you have background in the C language and Unix, Linux should feel like home to you.

Linux offers you the basic tools that you may have experienced using on a Unix workstation, such as Sun Microsystems, HP (Hewlett-Packard), and IBM.

6. Online documentation

After some time, you will want to look up more information about Linux without having to pull up this book. Fortunately, Linux has enough information published online that can help you in situations such as recalling a syntax for a command. To pull this information up quickly, all you need to do us to type in "man" in the command line to get the manual page for Linux commands. You can also get help from your desktop and use either the help option or icon.

Things to Consider When Choosing Distros

What is the best Linux distro (short for distribution) is for you? Here are some things that you may want to keep in mind:

1. Package managers

One of the major factors that separate distros from one another is the package manager that they come with. Just like what you may expect, there are distros that come with features that allow them to be easier to use from the command line while you are installing the features that come with them.

Another thing that you need to consider apart from the ease of use is the package availability that comes with distros. For example, there are certain distros that are not as popular as the others, which means that there are less apps out there that are developed to be used with certain distributions. If you are starting out on Linux, it may be a good idea to install a distro that does not only promise easy navigation from the get-go, but also a wide range of apps that you may want to install in the future.

2. Desktop environment

You will want to have a distro that allows you to enjoy a desktop that works well with your computing needs – you will definitely want a desktop that has great customization options, and easy to find windows and menus. You will also want to ensure that your desktop have efficient resource usage, as well as great integration with the apps that you plan to use.

While it is possible for you to place another desktop environment in the future, you will still want the desktop that comes with your distro to resemble the desktop that you really want to have. This way, you will not have to spend too much effort trying to setup every app that you want to have quick access to and ensure that all your applications are able to work well as they run together.

3. Hardware Compatibility

Different distros contain different drivers in the installation package that they come from, which means that there is a recommended set of hardware for them to work seamlessly. Of course, you can check out other sources of drivers that will work best with your existing hardware, but that only creates more work when it comes to getting everything running right away from installation. To prevent this trouble, check the distro's compatibility page and see whether all your computer peripherals work fine with your Linux distribution out of the box.

4. Stability and Being Cutting Edge

Different distributions put different priorities on stability and updates to get the latest version of applications and packages. For example, the distro Debian tends to delay getting some application updates to make sure that your operating system remains stable. This may not be suitable for certain users that prefer to always get the latest version of applications and get the latest features.

Fedora, on the other hand, performs quite the opposite – it is focused on getting all your programs and features up to date and ensures that you always have the greatest and the latest wares for your Linux. However, this may happen at the expense of stability of the app, which may prompt you to roll back to the previous version.

5. Community Support

Linux is all about the community that continuously provides support to this operating system, from documentation to troubleshooting. This means that you are likely to get the resources that you need when it comes to managing a particular distribution if it has a large community.

Great Distros to Try

Now that you know what makes a Linux distribution great and you are about to shop for the distro that you are going to install, you may want to check these distributions that may just work well for you:

1. Ubuntu

Ubuntu is largely designed to make Linux easy to use for an average computer user, which makes it a good distribution for every beginner. This distro is simple, updates every six months, and has a Unity interface, which allows you to use features such as a dock, a store-like interface for the package manager, and a dashboard that allows you to easily find anything on the OS. Moreover, it also comes with a standard set of applications that works well with most users, such as a torrent downloader, a Firefox web browser, and an app for instant messaging. You can also expect great support from its large community.

2. Linux Mint

This distro is based on Ubuntu, but is designed to make things even easier for any user that has not used Linux in the past – it features familiar menus and is not limited to just making you use open source programs. This means that you can get programs that are standard in popular operating systems such as .mp3 support and Adobe Flash, as well as a number of proprietary drivers.

3. Debian

If you want to be cautious and you want to see to it that you are running a bug-free and stable computer at all times, then this is probably the distro for you. Its main thrust is to make Linux a completely reliable system, but this can have some drawbacks –Debian does not prioritize getting the latest updates for applications that you have, which means that you may have to manually search for the latest release of most software that you own. The upside is that you can run Debian on numerous processor architectures and it is very likely to run on old builds.

However, this does not mean that going with Debian is having to remain outdated – it has a lot of programs available online and in Linux repositories.

4. OpenSUSE

OpenSUSE is a great distro that you may consider trying out because it allows you to configure your OS without having the need to deal with the command line. It usually comes with the default desktop KDE, but will also let you select between LXDE, KDE, XFCE, and GNOME as you install the distro package. It also provides you good documentation, the YaST package manager, and great support from the community.

One of the drawbacks that you may have when using this distro is that it can consume a lot of resources, which means that it is not ideal to use on older processor models and netbooks.

5. Arch Linux

Arch Linux is the distro for those that want to build their operating system from scratch. All that you are going to get from the installation package from the start is the command line, which you will use to get applications, desktop environment, drivers, and so on. This means that you can aim to be as minimal or as heavy in features, depending on what your needs are.

If you want to be completely aware of what is inside your operating system, then Arch Linux is probably the best distro for you to start with. You will be forced to deal with any possible errors that you may get, which can be a great way to learn about operating Linux.

Another thing that makes this distro special is that it uses Pacman, which is known to be a powerful package manager. Pacman comes in a rolling release, which means that you are bound to install the latest version of every package that is included – this ensures that you are bound to get cutting edge applications and features for your Linux. Apart from this package manager, you also get to enjoy the AUR (Arch User Repository), which allows you to create installable version of available programs. This means that if you want a program that is not available in Arch repositories, you can use the AUR helper to install applications and other features like normal packages.

When you run the command by pressing Enter on the keyboard, you get feedback as a text. It is through command line that we are presented with a prompt. This means that as you type the command, it will be displayed after the prompt. In most cases, you will be issuing the command. For instance:

user@bash:**ls -l** /home/Gary

total 3

drwxr-xr-x 2 Gary users 4096 Mar 23 13:34 bin

drwxr-xr-x 18 Gary users 4096 Feb 17 09:12 Documents

drwxr-learned-x 2 Gary users 4096 May 05 17:25 public html

user@bash:

74

To break this content down:

Line 1: this presents the prompt to us as user bash. Once we have the prompt, we are supposed to enter a command, in this case, ls. This means that typically, a command is the first thing that we have to type. After which, we are supposed to key in an argument in the command line (-l/home/Gary). In this case, the first thing that you have to bear in mind is that these are separated by spaces. That is, after typing the command, then you put in space before you can type in the argument. The first argument that we have used in this case **-l** is also referred to as an option. Options play a significant role in modifying the behavior of a command. They are often listed before other arguments, and they begin with a dash (-)

Line 2-5: These represent the outputs that we get once we run the commands we keyed in. Most of the commands that we key into the terminal will yield outputs that will be listed immediately after the command. However, there are other commands that when you run them, they will not display the results or any information unless in cases of error.

Line 6: This presents the prompt once again. Once you run the command that you typed into the terminal, and you have the results after running the command, you get a prompt. This means that if the prompt is not displayed after running a certain command, then this indicates that the command is still running. One important thing that I want you to know is that while on a terminal, you might not have the numberings on each line. This was just for me to explain what each line represents.

How then do we open a terminal?

When working with Linux, the first thing that you have to learn is to know how to open a terminal. It is fairly easy. It is kind of hard to tell you how to do it based on the fact that every system is different. However, some of the few places that you can begin are these:

If you are using Mac, the first thing you do is go to applications and then click on utilities. Under utilities, you have a terminal option which you select, and there you have a working terminal to type your commands. Alternatively, the best and easiest key combinations to opening a Linux terminal is "command + space." This combination will bring up a spotlight where you will type terminal and it will soon after show up on the screen. You can also download MobaXterm and use it on   Mac (http://macdownload.informer.com/macterm/download /) as a local terminal.

If you are working on Linux, then you will be able to access a terminal by clicking on systems and then applications. Under applications, you select utilities and select the terminal option. Alternatively, you can do this by simply right-clicking on a blank space on the desktop, and a drop down menu will appear. Select the "open in terminal" option, and there you are!

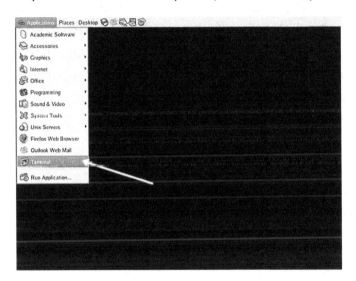

If you are using Windows, there are some ways you can use a terminal. The best one is using an SSH client to access the Linux terminal where you can run your commands. Some examples of application software that will allow you to do this are MobaXterm (http://download.cnet.com/MobaXterm/3000-7240_4-10890137.html) and Putty (http://www.putty.org/). With this software, the first thing is to download them online and install them on your Pc. On the desktop, you will have the shortcut that you can click on every time you need the terminal.

In most cases, it is not considered a great idea to use the root account for normal tasks. In other words, it is the root account that often plays a significant role when the user is running privileged commands as well as while maintaining the system. Therefore, for you to create a user account, the first important step is to log in to the root and use the **useradd** or **adduser** command. When using the Windows MobaXterm or Putty application, you simply click on the shortcut on your desktop, and a window terminal will appear. Then you will be prompted to log in as follows:

1. user@bash: **ssh** Gary@hpc.ucdavis.edu.uk
2. Unauthorized access is prohibited.
3. **<u>ssh</u>**   **<u>Gary@hpc.ucdavis.edu.uk's</u>** **Password:**
4. Last login: Fri Feb 17 14:34:27 2017 from 40.290.160.11

Once you enter the account username, the system will prompt you to key in a password for that account as shown above. When you are entering the password, the characters that you are typing will not be echoed to the screen. This means that you have to type very carefully. The main reason is that when you mistype the password, you will need a message log in incorrect, and this means that you have to try again. Once you have entered the password correctly for your account, then you are free to access the files and directories in that account.

The Shell, Bash

Within the terminal, there is a shell. This is part of the operating system that plays a significant role in defining the manner in which the terminal will behave. It also looks after execution of commands for you. There is a broad range of shells available, but the most common one is referred to as bash. This denotes "**Bourne again shell**." This Linux tutorial will make the assumption that you are using bash as your shell. However, if you wish to know what shell you are using, then the best thing to do is use the command echo. This command plays an important role in displaying a system variable that states the current shell in use. In other words, the command echo is used to display messages. As long as everything that it prints on the screen ends with the term bash, then you know that all is well.

1. user@bash: **echo $SHELL**
2. /bin/bash
3. user@bash:

Shortcuts

One of the most important shortcuts is using the up and down arrow key on your keyboard. When you are typing commands on Linux, they are kept in a history. The simplest way you can traverse this history is using these two keys. This means that the commands that you have used before do not need any retyping. You simply hit the up arrow a few times to get the command that you are looking for. Additionally, to edit the commands that you have used before, you can use the left and right arrow keys to move the cursor to where you need to perform edits.

There are times that you will notice that something is not working right while you are in a GUI desktop environment – there are times wherein a program crashes and the entire system refuses to respond to mouse clicks. There are even situations wherein the GUI may not start at all. When you run into trouble, you can still tell your operating system what to do, but you will have to do it using a text screen or the shell, which serves as the command interpreter for Linux.

Since Linux is essentially a Unix program, you will be doing a lot of tasks using the text terminal. Although the desktop will be doing the job of providing you the convenience to access anything through a click of the mouse, there are several occasions wherein you need to access the terminal.

Learning how to enter commands will save you from a lot of trouble when you encounter an X Window system error, which is the program that controls all the menus and the windows that you see in your desktop GUI. To fix this error, or to prevent it from stopping you to access the program or file that you want, you can pull up a terminal and enter a command instead. In the future, you might want to keep a terminal open in your desktop since it can make you order your computer faster than having to point and click.

The Bash Shell

If you have used the MS-DOS OS in the past, then you are familiar with command.com, which serves as the command interpreter for DOS. In Linux, this is called the shell. The default shell in all the different distros, is called the bash.

Bourne-Again Shell, or bash, is capable of running any program that you have stored in your computer as an executable file. It can also run shell scripts, or a text files that are made up of Linux commands. In short, this shell serves as a command interpreter, or a program that interprets anything that you type as a command and performs what this input is supposed to do.

Pulling up the terminal window can be as simple as clicking on a monitor-looking icon on the desktop – clicking on it will lead you to a prompt. If you can't find that icon, simply search through the Main menu and select the item with has the Terminal or Console label.

Tip: You have the choice to use other shells apart from the bash, just like you have a choice in choosing desktops. You can always change the shell that you are using for your distro by entering the chsh command on the terminal.

The Shell Command

Every shell command follows this format:

```
command option1 option2 . . . optionN
```

A command line, such as a command that follows the above format, is typically followed by parameters (also known as arguments). When entering a command line, you need to enter a space to separate the main command from the options and to separate one option from another. However, if you want to use an option that contains a space in its syntax, you will need to enclose that option in quotation marks. Take a look at this example:

```
grep "Emmett Dulaney" /etc/passwd
```

The grep command allowed you to find for a particular text in a file, which is Emmett Dulaney in this case. Once you press enter, you will get the following result:

```
edulaney:x:1000:100:Emmett Dulaney:/home/edulaney:/bin/bash
```

If you want to read a particular file, you can use the "more" command. Try entering this command:

```
more /etc/passwd
```

You will be getting a result that appears like this:

```
root:x:0:0:root:/root:/bin/bash
bin:x:1:1:bin:/bin:/bin/bash
daemon:x:2:2:Daemon:/sbin:/bin/bash
lp:x:4:7:Printing daemon:/var/spool/lpd:/bin/bash
mail:x:8:12:Mailer daemon:/var/spool/clientmqueue:/bin/false
news:x:9:13:News system:/etc/news:/bin/bash
uucp:x:10:14:Unix-to-Unix Copy system:/etc/uucp:/bin/bash
 . . . lines deleted . . .
```

83

To see all programs are running on your computer, use the "ps" command. Try entering this command on the terminal:

```
ps ax
```

The options ax (option a lists all running processes, while opion x shows the rest of the proceses) allows you to see all the processes that are available in your system, which looks like this:

```
PID TTY STAT TIME COMMAND
1 ? S 0:01 init [5]
2 ? SN 0:00 [ksoftirqd/0]
3 ? S< 0:00 [events/0]
4 ? S< 0:00 [khelper]
9 ? S< 0:00 [kthread]
22 ? S< 0:00 [kblockd/0]
58 ? S 0:00 [kapmd]
79 ? S 0:00 [pdflush]
80 ? S 0:00 [pdflush]
82 ? S< 0:00 [aio/0]
. . . lines deleted . . .
5325 ? Ss 0:00 /opt/kde3/bin/kdm
5502 ? S 0:12 /usr/X11R6/bin/X -br -nolisten tcp :0 vt7 -auth
      /var/lib/xdm/authdir/authfiles/A:0-p1AOrt
5503 ? S 0:00 -:0
6187 ? Ss 0:00 /sbin/portmap
6358 ? Ss 0:00 /bin/sh /usr/X11R6/bin/kde
6566 ? Ss 0:00 /usr/sbin/cupsd
6577 ? Ss1 0:00 /usr/sbin/nscd
. . . lines deleted . . .
```

The amount of the command-line options and their corresponding formats would depend on the actual command. These options appear like the –X, wherein X represents one character. For esampe, you can opt to use the option –l for the ls command, which will list a directory's contents. Take a look at what happens when you enter the command ls –l in the home directory for a user:

```
total 0
drwxr-xr-x 2 edulaney users 48 2014-09-08 21:11 bin
drwx------ 2 edulaney users 320 2014-09-08 21:16 Desktop
drwx------ 2 edulaney users 80 2014-09-08 21:11 Documents
drwxr-xr-x 2 edulaney users 80 2014-09-08 21:11 public_html
drwxr-xr-x 2 edulaney users 464 2014-09-17 18:21 sdump
```

If you enter a command that is too long to be contained on a single line, press the \ (backslash) key and then hit Enter. Afterwards, go on with the rest of the command on the following line. Try typing the following command and hit Enter when you type a line:

```
cat \
/etc/passwd
```

This will display all the contents inside the /ets/passwd file.

You can also string together (also known as concatenate) different short commands on one line by separating these commands with the ; (semicolon) symbol. Take a look at this command:

```
cd; ls -l; pwd
```

This command will make you jump to your user's home directory, show the contents of the directory you shanged into, and then display the name of the current directory.

Putting Together Your Shell Commands

If you are aiming to make a more sophisticated command, such as finding out whether you have a file named sbpcd in the /dev directory because you need that file for your CD drive, you can opt to combine different commands to make the entire process shorter. What you can do is that you can enter the ls /dev command to show the contents of the /dev directory and see if it contains the file that you want.

However, you may also get too many entries in the /dev directory when the command returns with the results. However, you can combine the grep command, which you have learned earlier, with the ls command and search for the exact file that you are looking for. Now, type in the following command:

```
ls /dev | grep sbpcd
```

This will show you the directory listing (result of the ls command) while the grep command searches for the string "sbpcd". The pipe (|) serves as the connection between the two separate commands that you use, wherein the first command's output is used as the input for the second one.

Command Substitution

A command standard's output can be encapsulated, pretty much the same way a value can be stored in a value, before then being expanded by the shell. This concept is known as command substitution.

Going by the bash documentation, command substitution basically allows a command's output to replace the command itself. In bash, the expansion is done by executing command and having the command substitution take the place of the command's standard output, with all the trailing newlines erased. The embedded newlines don't get erased, but during word splitting, they may be deleted.

Let's take an example:

Consider the command 'seq'. It will print a sequence of numbers beginning from the first argument to the second one as follows:

user@host~:$ seq 1 5

1

2

3

4

5

Command substitution can help you encapsulate the 'seq 1 5' result into a variable. This is through enclosing the command with $(and), and passing it as an argument to a different command.

user@host~:$ echo $(seq 1 5)

1 2 3 4 5

Or, to create 5 new directories:

user@host~:$ mkdir $(seq 1 5)

Variables And Command Expansion

Sometimes a command is replaced by its standard output; the output, which, presumably, is just text, can therefore be assigned to a variable just like any other value:

user@host~:$ a=$(echo 'hello' | tr '[:lower:]' '[:upper:]')

user@host~:$ b=$(echo 'WORLD' | tr '[:upper:]' '[:lower:]')

user@host~:$ echo "$a, $b"

HELLO, world

When Newlines Are Omitted

I earlier noted something from the bash documentation.

Let me give you a deeper version of that excerpt:

With command substitution, the command output is able to replace the command itself. Bash executes the command and replaces command substitution with the command's standard output- that is how it performs the expansion. Note that at the same time, any trailing newlines are deleted. The embedded newlines don't get removed, but as I mentioned earlier, they may be deleted during the process of word splitting.

In case you're wondering what that means, consider 'seq 1 5' being called as it normally would, and then, through command substitution, and take note of how the formatting changes.

```
user@host:~$ seq 1 5

1

2

3

4

5
user@host:~$ echo $(seq 1 5)

1 2 3 4 5
```

But why are the newlines getting removed during the command expansion? This is something we'll experience later; it's all about the way bash essentially interprets space and newline characters during the expansion. In any case, you may want to note the behavior for now, because it may be new to you if you're particularly coming from a different programming language.

Word-Splitting In The Wild

This is a short section on how bash deals with space characters when it performs an expansion.

Given that many people are used to copying and pasting code directly from the internet, it's worth knowing the various ways you could harm yourself without knowing it. This is due to the manner in which bash handles spaces and newline characters.

The Internal Field Separator

The Internal field separator 'IFS' is used by bash to split strings into distinct words. You can think of it as the way excel splits a comma-separated-values (CSV) text file into spreadsheets; according to it, commas separate the columns.

We'll assume that IFS is set to something arbitrary, such as Z. When a variable is expanded by bash, which contains a 'Z', that value's variable will be split into distinct words (in that case, the literal Z disappears):

user@host:~$ IFS=Z

user@host:~$ story="The man named Zorro r

user@host:~$ echo '>>' $story '<<'

>> The man named orro rides a ebra <<

The IFS variable is by default set to three characters, which include space, tab and newline. If you echo '$IFS', you will not be able to see anything since, obviously, it wouldn't be possible to see a space character without any visible characters. So what is the upshot? Simple, you may see snippets of code online in which the variable 'IFS' is changed to $ '\n' (this stands for 'newline character') or something similar.

Imagine having a text file that has a set of lines of text, which, for instance, may refer to filenames as follows:

rough draft.tx

draft 1.txt

draft 2.txt

final draft.txt

When each line of the file is read, the IFS' default value (which definitely includes a space character), causes bash to treat the file: 'rough draft . txt' as a double or two files which are 'rough' and 'draft . txt', this is because splitting words uses the space character.

When IFS is set to the newline character, the 'rough draft . txt' becomes treated as one filename.

As you will notice, this concept will make sense when it comes to reading text files and operating on each and every line. It might not be possible to understand this fully but you it is important you become aware of it, at least just in case you're used to copy-pasting code from the internet haphazardly.

How Bad Can Unquoted Variables Be?

In a nice, ideal world, we all would keep our string values short and devoid of space or newlines, and any other special characters. In such a world, the unquoted variable reference below would work perfectly:

```
user@host:~$ file_to_kill='whatsup.txt'
usr@host:~$ rm $file_to_kill   # delete the file named whatsup.txt
```

However, when we start adding special characters to filenames, like spaces and expanding variables without using double quotes, it can be detrimental. In the example below, I want the file by the name 'junk final.docx' deleted:

```
user@host:~$ file_to_kill='Junk Final.docx'
```

Unanticipated word-splitting

Nonetheless, when referenced without double quotes, bash perceives 'file_to_kill' as one that has two separate values that include 'junk' and 'final.docx' below:

```
user@host:~$ file_to_kill='Junk Final.docx'
user@host:~$ rm $file_to_kill
rm: cannot remove 'Junk': No such file or directory
rm: cannot remove 'Final.docx': No such file or directory
```

Unanticipated special characters

You might think, "but there's no harm done" because those files did not even exist in the first place. That's fine, but what would happen if someone placed an asterisk into a filename? You do know what happens when someone does 'grep *' and 'rm *' don't you? The star acts like a hungry bear, grabbing all the files.

```
user@host:~$ file_to_kill='Junk * Final.docx'
user@host:~$ rm $file_to_kill
```

Given that 'junk' and 'final.docx' are nonexistent, you'll be able to see the previous errors. However, in between those tried deletions, 'rm' runs on the asterisk. So, just say goodbye to all the files in that directory.

You do see how 'rm "$filename" only affects the file named '* LOL BYE FILES'. Therefore, the main takeaway here is **always use double quotes in your variable references as often as you can.**

Here's a little more info that you deserve...

You might be thinking 'who in the world would place a star character in their filename?' For one, we do have folks who enjoy star-shaped symbols; also, we have malicious hackers and annoying prank-stars who wouldn't mind using a star character. Note that variables are usually not just assigned as a result of human typing; as you already know, at times, the result of commands are stored in a variable. In the instance raw data is being processed by such commands, it is possible that that kind of data does contain special characters that can damage certain bash programs.

You always have to keep it in mind the dangers of just pasting in code that seems safe. The syntax and behavior of bash in handling strings is quite difficult to understand, which is why developers turn to other languages to go about more complex applications.

From all that reading, I think you need a little break. Take a time-out by going through some basic aspects of bash that will help you in the next chapter, which are numeric and string comparisons.

Linux allows you to make use of different commands, as well as the ability to connect these commands, which has been discussed in a previous chapter. You have also learned how to make use of I/O redirection and pipes. The Bourne-Again Shell or bash, allows you to also use of the IF condition, which means that you can only run a program when you meet certain conditions. All the features of the bash can be used to create your own programs, or shell scripts. Shell scripts are known as shell command collections that perform tasks, which are then stored in a file.

In this chapter, you will learn how to create simple shell scripts that can be extremely useful in automating various tasks in Linux.

Creating Your First Script

Shell scripting, which is also called programming, can be daunting to anyone who has not tried out any programming language in the past. However, you might find learning how to program can be easy because you have already tried out different commands during the earlier chapters of this book.

If you are a system administrator, you can actually create an entire collection of custom-made scripts that will help you perform your tasks easier. For example, if there is a hard drive that is about to become full, you may want to automatically find all files that go beyond a particular size and has not been accessed by any user for a month. You may also want to create a script that will be automatically be sent to all users that own large files, so that they can be informed that they need to set up their archives and remove those files from your network's shared resources. All these tasks can actually be done with a single script.

First, you will need to use the find command to search for all the large files in your system:

```
find / -type f -atime +30 -size +1000k -exec ls -l {} \; > /tmp/largefiles
```

Using the above command will create a file called /tmp/largefiles, which will contain all the information that you need about the old files that are occupying too much drive space. Once you get the list of all these files, you can make use of some Linux commands, such as sed, sort, and cut, to set up and send your email message to the users who own these large files.

Of course, you will want to not waste your time and type out all these commands one by one. What you want to do is to do all these tasks by creating a shell script that have these commands. A bash script will allow you to include all these command options, which you can refer to as $1, $2, etc. The characters $0 is reserved for the name of the script that you have created. Take a look at this sample bash script:

```
#!/bin/sh
echo "This script's name is: $0"
echo Argument 1: $1
echo Argument 2: $2
```

This script's first line will run the program /bin/sh, which will then process all the remaining lines in this script. The /bin/sh is also the Bourne shell, which is known as Unix's first shell. In Linux, /bin/sh links to the /bin/bash, which is the bash's executable program.

Now, save the above script with the filename simple and then turn it into an executable file by entering this command:

```
chmod +x simple
```

Now, run the script using this command:

```
./simple
```

You will see this output:

```
This script's name is: ./simple
Argument 1:
Argument 2:
```

You will notice that the first line in the output displays the script's name. Because there is no argument in the

97

script, the output will also not display any value for the arguments.

Now, you can run the script again, but include arguments this time:

```
./simple "This is one argument" second-argument third
```

The output will appear like this:

```
This script's name is: ./simple
Argument 1: This is one argument
Argument 2: second-argument
```

As you can see, the shell considers the entire string inside the quotation marks as a single argument. Without it, the shell will consider the spaces to separate the arguments in the command line. Because your script did not say that it also needs to print more than two arguments, the third argument is left from the output.

Shell Scripting Basics

The shell script supports features that are also present in other programming languages:

- **Variables, or objects that store values. This includes built-in variables that are accessible to command line arguments.**

- **Use of control structures that will allow you to loop over commands**

- **Ability to use conditional commands**

- **Ability to evaluate expressions**

98

- **Ability to use functions and to call them in different places in your script.**

Storing with Variables

In bash, you can define variables in this manner:

```
count=12 # note no embedded spaces allowed
```

When you have already defined the value of a variable, you can use the prefix $. For example, the variable PATH has a value of $PATH. Now, if you want to show the value for the variable count, enter:

```
echo $count
```

bash uses a few special variables when it comes to using command-line arguments. For example, the variable $* will store all arguments in the command line as a single variable, and the $? will serve as the container for the exit status when the shell executes the last command in the script.

In a bash script, you can tell the user to key in a value that you require and then use the read command to turn that into a variable's value. Take a look at this sample script:

```
echo -n "Enter value: "
read value
echo "You entered: $value"
```

When you run this script, the command read value will prompt bash to read all the things that the user enters and then store that input into a variable that is named value. Take note that the −n option in this sample script is added to prevent the echo command from adding a new line at the string's end automatically.

Calling Functions

You can lump together a group of commands into a function with an assigned name, and then use them during different areas in your script. Once you have commands grouped into a function, you can simply key in the function's name to execute all the commands that was assigned to it. Take a look at this sample script:

```
#!/bin/sh
hello() {
echo -n "Hello, "
echo $1 $2
}
hello Jane Doe
```

Running this script will give you this output:

```
Hello, Jane Doe
```

Controlling the Scrip Flow

You can have control of how the script will execute the commands that you have indicated by using special commands. Commands like *if*, *while*, *case*, and *for* allows you to use a command's exit status and then do the next action. When a command is executed, it gives an exit status, or a numerical value that indicates whether you have succeeded in executing the command. By programming convention, having an exit status of zero means that the command has been accomplished.

For example, you want to make a copy of a file before you pull up the vi editor to make some changes to the file. At the same time you also want to make it a point that no changes are going to be made to the file if the backup file is not created. To take care of all these tasks, you can use the following script:

```
#!/bin/sh
if cp "$1" "#$1"
then
vi "$1"
else
echo "Failed to create backup copy"
fi
```

This script shows the syntax of the structure if-then-else and also displays how the cp command's exit status by the if command, which determines what the next action is going to be. If the cp displays an exit status of zero, you will have access to vi to edit the file. If that is not the case, the script will show you an error message and then exits. Also take note that the script will save the backup file that you have requested using the same filename, but with a hashtag at the beginning of the backup file's name.

Also take note that you need to enter the command fi to let the script know that you have ended the if command. Otherwise, you will encounter an error in your script.

If you want to evaluate any expression and also use the value of the expression to serve as a command's exit status, the test command is going to be handy for that task. For example, if you want to create a script that will only edit an existing file, you can use the test command in this manner:

```
#'/bin/sh
if test -f "$1"
then
vi "$1"
else
echo "No such file"
fi
```

Take note that you can also use a shorter test command by using the square bracket ([ ]) to contain the expression. You can edit the above sample script to look like this:

```
#!/bin/sh
if [ -f "$1" ]
then
vi "$1"
else
echo "No such file"
fi
```

Another control structure that you can use is the for loop. Take a look at how this control structure is used in this script that Is designed to add the numbers 1 through 10:

103

```
#!/bin/sh
sum=0
for i in 1 2 3 4 5 6 7 8 9 10
do
sum='expr $sum + $i'
done
echo "Sum = $sum"
```

Take note that the above script also showed how the expr command was used to evaluate an expression.

If you want to execute a command group according to variable value, the case statement is going to be useful. Take a look at this example script:

```
#!/bin/sh
echo -n "What should I do -- (Y)es/(N)o/(C)ontinue? [Y] "
read answer
case $answer in
y|Y|"")
echo "YES"
;;
c|C)
echo "CONTINUE"
;;
n|N)
echo "NO"
;;
*)
echo "UNKNOWN"
;;
esac
```

Now, save this script as confirm, and then enter this command to turn it into an executable file:

chmod +x confirm

When the script prompts you for a requested action, press any of these keys: Y, N, or C. This is how the output will look like:

```
What should I do -- (Y)es/(N)o/(C)ontinue? [Y] c
CONTINUE
```

The script stores your input into the variable answer, and the case statement runs a code according to the value of your input. For example, if you press the C key, this code block will run:

```
c|C)
echo "CONTINUE"
;;
```

As the code's output, the text CONTINUE is displayed.

Take a look at another example to see how the case command's syntax is used:

```
case $variable in
value1 | value2)
command1
command2
. . . other commands . . .
;;
value3)
command3
command4
. . . other commands . . .
;;
esac
```

You will notice that the case command starts with the word case and then terminates with the word esac. There are also code blocks that are contained within the variable values, which were followed by a closing parenthesis. When all other commands for the script are already entered, they are ended with two semicolons.

Chapter 5 : Acquainted with the linux file system and processes

Linux's file system is outstanding when it comes to flexibility. Its design allows it to support regular, as well as special types of file formats. It can support text, programs, images, services, output, and input devices. Therefore, since it supports a variety of file formats, it can coexist with another OS.

Moreover, in the system, there is hardly a distinguishable factor between a file and a directory. It follows that directions are simply locations of file stacks.

File system

Categorization of Files

To ensure better understanding of the Linux file system, files are categorized. While it is considerably safe to assume, knowing more information about a particular file allows programmers and system administrators to avoid complexities when using Linux. This also prevents them from performing long listings.

File categories:

- Directory (d) – a file that is a list of a stack of files

- Link (l) – a system that allows the visibility of a particular file in multiple parts of a file tree

- Pipe (p) – a system that allows inter-process communication

- Regular (-) – a normal file

- Socket (s) – a special file that provides inter-process networking

- Special (c) – a mechanism used for output and input

The Art of Partitioning

Partitioning in Linux began when power failures threatened majority of Linux users. There were days when an outage meant serious damages to a system.

Moreover, a primary reason for partitioning is to achieve a much higher data security level. The hard disk's division allows safe grouping and protection.

Due to successful partitioning, you can prioritize data groups with more importance. When part of a hard disk is compromised, only that part of the disk is affected. The rest that are stored in other partitions remains untouched.

Two major partitions in a Linux system:

1. Swap – refers to extra memory or an expansion

2. Data – refers to normal data; refers to the necessities for starting and running a system

Recommended partitions:

- A partition for necessary data

- A partition for server programs and configuration data

- A partition for programs and applications

- At least one partition for user mails, archives, and database tables

- At least one partition for specific files

- At least one partition for virtual memory

Common partitions:

- A partition that contains personal data

- A partition that stores temporary files

- A partition that stores third party data

- A partition that is solely for programs

Directories: The Root Directory & Subdirectories

In Linux, there is a directory called **The Root Directory**. It serves as the main directory and as programmers and system administrators would refer to it, it is the directory of all directories.

With The Root Directory come the subdirectories. These subdirectories manage files according to their assigned tasks.

Subdirectories and their content:

- /home – home directory

- /boot – the kernel and startup files; files that attempt to eliminate unnecessary bootloaders

- /initrd – data regarding booting information

- /dev – contains references to all CPU hardware peripherals

- /bin – common shared system programs

- /etc – important systems configuration data

- /lib – library files

- /lost+found – retrieved data from failures

- /opt – files from third party sources

- /net – remote file systems' standard mount point

- /misc – miscellaneous data

- /proc – information regarding system resources

- /mnt – external file systems' standard mount point

The Role of an Inode

In a Linux file system, an **inode** represents a file. An inode is a type of serial number that contains important information. Its primary role revolves around defining the number of files in a partition.

Throughout a Linux file system, especially one with multiple partitions, there are files with similar inode. To avoid complications, each partition is assigned its own inode.

Moreover, an assigned inode provides a description of a hard disk's data structure. Once a hard disk's initialization is finished, it can accept data storage during two points. One, data storage is acceptable during the installation process. Two, data storage is acceptable upon the addition of storage space to an existing system.

Information contained in an inode:

- File type

- File size

- Owner or group owner of the file

- Date and time of creation

- Date and time of latest modification

- Permissions

- Number of links

- Data address

What Is The Superblock?

In Linux's file system, the information about basic file size and shape is called **The Superblock**. It allows a file system manager to peruse and maintain a file system's quality.

Information in The Superblock:

- Free blocks – displays the number of a system's free blocks

- Free inode – shows the original inode assignment

- Free inodes – displays the number of a system's free inodes

- Block group number – refers to a number assigned to The superblock

- Blocks per group - displays a group's number of blocks

- Block size – refers to a system's block size; information is shown in bytes

- Magic number – refers to the permission granted to mounting software for assessment

- Mount count – refers to a system's allowance for assessment

- Revision level – refers to a system's allowance for revision level confirmation

What Is a Group Descriptor?

A **group descriptor** is in charge of labeling a file's data structure. It contains details to avoid duplication of data. Due to its role, a system's possibility of corruption is minimal.

Information in a group descriptor:

- Blocks bitmap

- Free blocks count

- Free inodes count

- Inode bitmap

- Inode table

- Used directory count

File Modification: Finding, Mounting & Changing Sizes

A Linux file is usually easy to locate. Just search for a directory and the name that succeeds a "/" or a forward slash might be your preferred file.

You can then start mounting. When mounting a file, the availability of a Linux kernel is necessary to check the standards. Its presence allows the validation of all of a system's passed arguments.

As the sample shows, you are mounting three kinds of information. "iso898", "/dev/rom", and "/dev/cdrom".

Apart from finding and mounting a file, you have the option to change a file's size. This is done due to the occurrence of a file's fragmentation.

Since files become inefficient during fragmentation, changing a file's size allows the allocation of files. Consequently, a system becomes more stable.

You are introduced to the commands "truncate" and "fallocate". Both commands allows you to create a file with a preferred size.

The Processes

Although it is considerably fair, Linux experiences errors occasionally. System administrators are aware of this. Especially if they regularly modify and manage programs according to their preferred design, they are no longer strangers to unexpected faults.

The program management of a Linux system is called a process.

What Is a Process?

As mentioned, a process is the program management of Linux. It refers to the running instances of programs.

Since Linux is capable of handling multiple tasks, it is typical for many processes to be run simultaneously. Alongside the initiated processes that are currently running, the OS is designed to run another batch of processes for general management.

Elements of a process:
- **Identifiers**

Identifiers are assigned numbers to every process in the system. Sometimes, they are mistaken as the index into a task vector, but they are simply numbers. They are meant to let users identify particular processes easily.

- **Inter-process communication**

The support for Linux's classic mechanisms of semaphores, signals, and pipes is called inter-process communication.

- **Links**

Links represent the inter-dependence of processes. With the exception of the initial process, every process in a Linux system has a parent process.

- **Scheduling information**

Scheduling information refers to information regarding fair decisions regarding the priority of processes.

- **State**

State refers to changes in process' execution.

A process' different states:

- o Waiting state

- o Running state

- o Zombie state

- o Stopped state

What Are Signals?

In Linux, some processes need manipulation. The mechanism for the manipulation of processes is called signals.

Signals serve as special messages that are relayed to processes. They are asynchronous. Once processes receive signals, the signals are interpreted almost immediately. Over running processes, they are prioritized.

There are instances when signals do not specify behavior. They are assigned one of three values, and these values determine responses. Be careful when assigning values to a signal, since these values can be corrupted when another signal is delivered.

Values:

- **SIG_IGN – says that signals should be ignored**

- **SIG_DFL – defines a default disposition**

- **Signal pointer (pointer to the signal-handler function) – takes a parameter, gets the signal number, and returns void**

The Creation of a Process

In Linux, the creation of a process is possible. The kernel is necessary and is assigned "1" as a process identifier. It begins with the selection of an old process, and this old process is cloned.

Since process creation necessitates the kernel, the cloning occurs in kernel mode. It allows two processes to be merged or use similar resources, rather than have processes' presentation as two similar copies.

All Running Processes: What It Takes to View Them?

In Linux, all running processes are viewable. To do so, learn about the process status command or the "ps" command.

The ps command displays the information on all running processes. It serves as a repetitive update of information. It provides details regarding a selection.

More importantly, it displays the PIDs (or Process Identification Numbers). The PIDs are automatically assigned numbers. To view running processes, simply type the ps command first.

Options for viewing processes:

-A or -e – for viewing all processes

Input:

ps –A

Or

#ps –e

-u (username) – for viewing all processes run by a particular user

Input (for the username "mikael307"):

#ps –u (mikael307)

top – for viewing a top program

Input:

#ps top

As the output shows, the initial process is "pid". Under is "apache" that has a sub-process "gnome". Under "apache" is "tree", and "devkit". "devkit" has sub-processes named "sys" and "dev".

Under "dev" are the processes "run" and "ceno". Then, to proceed with the Initial "pid" process are "ff" and "log".

Killing a Process

Killing a process is an option. You can kill any process immediately to rid the system of a big load. It is done if you refuse to wait for a process' complete execution.

When using a non-Linux OS, logging out or restarting the computer is necessary to kill a running process. In Linux, simply type in particular commands and your preferred running processes will be terminated.

"#kill" is a Linux commands that delivers signals to kill particular processes. It can be either internal or external. If no signal is delivered by the command, "term" signals are the alternative.

Term signals:

- **Sigkill – kills a process without saving data; typically used as last resort**

- **Sigterm – safest and most practical term signal**

- **Sighup - reloads confirmation files; opens or closes the system's log files**

Killing a running process begins by knowing PIDs. In retrospect (Chapter 3, III), PIDs are assigned automatically during the creation of a process. To determine the PID of a process, simply type in "#pidof" followed by a process name.

Moreover, when killing a process, remember a few rules. While you can kill all of your own processes, you cannot invade other users' processes. Only the root user is permitted to kill a system-level process.

Steps in killing a running process:

1. Determine the PID of the process.

2. Use "# kill" command.

3. Type the PID of the process.

There's a "#killall" command, too. It serves useful if you want to kill a particular process and all its sub-processes.

The Role of the Fork & Exec Functions

A **fork** is the term used for a duplicate process. It is the replica of a parent process. Its use is to mimic a process, but operate on a different program.

Exec is a function that replaces the running programs in a process with other programs. When processes call exec, programs are immediately terminated. Upon termination of the original programs, replacements are launched. Given that exec does not encounter errors, replacement programs will continue running.

Reminders when using exec:

- Functions that include "p" in their names (e.g. execlp and execvp) are designed to accept and search for other programs in the current path

- Functions that include "e" in their names (e.g. execle and execve) are designed to accept additional arguments

- Functions that contain "v" in their names (e.g. execlv and execvp) are designed to accept argument lists for new programs

When used together, fork and exec can support a long process. First, a process is executed. Then, a sub-program is continued. It means that execution can go on, instead of terminating a process, in favor of a new one.

Chapter 6 : Common syntax across most linux distribution

The next thing you have to do is choose your own Linux Distribution. Basically, these are just the different versions of Linux that you can choose from, and yes, all of them are the same, when it comes to being Operating Systems, but they differ when it comes to aesthetics, and the way they "work".

Basically, there are various distributions to choose from, but there are seven that are the most trusted, and these are:

Ubuntu

Ubuntu is possibly one of the most popular distributions of Linux, and is deemed to be the best to choose if you're new to Linux, or have not tried it before. Ubuntu has amazing easy-to-install repositories, and is quite customizable—perfect for art and media practitioners, or those who are just extremely careful about what they see onscreen. The problem with Ubuntu is that compared to other distributions, it does not work as great with mobile devices—which can be a bit of a problem, especially if you're the type who's on your mobile device all the time.

Souls

Souls has that modern feel, and is in fact, somewhat new as it was released only in 2012—a time when Ubuntu was mostly used in schools and businesses. Some say that the best thing about Souls is its aesthetic feel, because it really has that elegant, nice-to-look-at feel to it. One thing, though, is that there aren't too many "Soul Communities" around yet, so if you get to have problems with this distribution, you might have to look for the solution yourself.

Mint Cinnamon

Such a fresh-sounding name, isn't it? Well, Mint Cinnamon actually has that fresh and light feel as it mostly makes use of white and gray for aesthetics. It's quite the minimalist distribution of Linux—perfect for people who do not like seeing a lot of pizzazz and anything too colorful on their screens. The best thing is that its repositories are the same as Ubuntu's, so you won't have much of a hard time trying to understand them, and its UI is also less-demanding—so it wouldn't be too taxing on your computer, and on you who's going to be using it. Mint Cinnamon is also deemed to be great for beginners, because as aforementioned, there's not much to understand about it—and you really don't have to give yourself a hard time for it, too.

Ubuntu Studio

As the name suggests, this incarnation of Linux is perfect for producers, musicians, sound engineers, designers, and artists who need to work with various kinds of multimedia, and who need computers or devices that are tailored for that purpose—Ubuntu Studio definitely makes that easy. Having been around since 2007, this one has a multi-track, digital recorder and sequencer named "Ardour" that's being relied on by many artists around the globe. The best thing about the said recorder is that it synthesizes guitar and other instruments that have been used, making sure that your final output would be really pleasing to the ears, and not at all hard to deal with. Therefore, you'd get to create projects that are of professional quality—without spending much for it.

Arch Linux

This one is deemed to be perfect for professionals because it is something that you have to work with and customize on your own. In fact, It does not even come with as many applications as other distributions do, which means that you do have to know what you're doing. With this, you have to apply the "Keep it Short and Simple" philosophy, because downloading too much might just make you confused. Find what you really want, and then prune or get rid of those you feel won't matter to you, so that your screen won't be too cramped, and so you can make the most out of this distribution. However, what's good about it is that you may learn a lot, so even if you may have a bit of a hard time in the beginning, rest assured, you'd get past that, and experience what Arch Linux really is about!

Chrome OS

It's said that this is one of the main and closest renditions of the early Linux GNU Kernel, but that it has actually exceeded expectations, and is proving to be one of the most reliable Linux distributions. It has since then been repurposed into a working environment on its own, mostly because it's used to make certain Google Apps, and works fast even if you use applications that take up much space, such as **Photoshop.** It will make your work much more manageable, but the issue is that there are certain applications that are not available on this distribution that you can find in other Linux distributions. It's also the kind of distribution that works better offline, so that could be hassle if you're always connected to the web, but you can make certain updates or upgrades with minimal fees, anyway.

Elementary OS

And finally, there's the Elementary Distribution. Not only is it one of the most aesthetically-pleasing versions of Linux, it's also highly functional, and some say has that resemblance to the Mac—perfect for multimedia artists and those who work with high-end applications, as well. In fact, it may as well be your perfect Windows or Mac replacement, in the event that you are looking for something new that you can rely on quite well. It also has an amazing line of pre-installed apps, and even a custom web-browser that can really personalize the way you use Linux.

How To Create Basic Scripts

As we've seen when you begin learning the command line interface, you generally explore it interactively. That means that you enter one command at a time so that you see the results of each one.

As we begin this section, you can first take a look at **this gif** (**http://bit.ly/2linux3**) which explores a

Shakespearean plays' directory using the command line; it counts the number of words and the frequency or how many times the term 'murder' appears in all the plays of Shakespeare.

It's totally fine to use the command-line interface in this interactive manner when you're trying out things but as you may likely notice, typing is one of those activities that are prone to errors. For tasks that are more complex i.e. tasks that you want to repeat, you don't want to retype the code right from the beginning, but make a self-contained shell script that's possible to run as a one-liner.

Your First Shell Script

We'll begin with something simple. Create a junk directory somewhere, like /tmp/my-playground. Your actual workspace doesn't have to be littered with test code.

A shell script is simply a text file that has to make sense. To create one, we'll use the nano text editor.

Nano?

Nano is a text editor. It comes preinstalled in nearly all Linux distros. New users prefer it mainly because of its simplicity, which stands out when compared to other command line text editors like emacs and vi/vim. It basically contains many other useful features like line numbering, syntax coloring and easy search (among others).

Let's continue.

We'll create a shell script called hello.sh. Just follow the following steps:

Type 'nano hello.sh' and run

Nano will open and give you a blank file to work in. Now enter the following shell command.

Echo 'hello world'

On your keyboard, press ctrl +x to exit the editor. When asked whether you want to save the file, press yes (y).

Nano will then confirm whether you want to save the file. Press enter to confirm the action.

Now run the script 'hello. sh' with the following command:

Bash hello.sh

When you look at it as a gif, the steps look something **like this**.

http://bit.ly/2piclinux

Therefore, 'hello.sh' is not particularly exciting, but at least it catches the essence of what you want to do, which is to wrap up a series of commands into a file, that is, a script, so that you can re-run the script as much as you'd want. That helps you remove the chance of having typographic errors that come about when

131

you're retyping commands, and also allows you to make the script reusable in various contexts.

Having Arguments In A Re-Usable Shell Script

Let's now try making 'hello. sh' a bit complicated. Now instead of repeating hello world, you'll create the script in such a way that it says 'hello' to a certain value- for instance, a person's name. That will make the script seem a bit better. You can use it like so:

```
bash hello.sh Dan

HELLO DAN
```

The gif is as **follows**.

http://bit.ly/2linux5

First off, you customize 'hello world' by adding a variable in the place of 'world'. Try to do that from the command line interactively:

```
yourname=Dan

echo "Hello $yourname"
```

The output is:

Hello Dan

Therefore, the question here is, how do you get the script 'hello.sh' to read in our argument (which is a person's name in this case) that you pass into it?

```
bash hello.sh George
```

You do that through a special bash variable. The first, second and third arguments you passed from the command line into the script are denoted by the variables which include $1, $2, $3. In the example above therefore, the name George will be kept in the variable $1 as 'hello.sh' starts running.

Just reopen 'hello.sh' and change your code to the following

```
$yourname – $1

echo "Hello $yourname"
```

After saving the changes, now run the following to see the output.

```
bash hello.sh Mary
```

If you desire to have the output returned in all caps, simply modify 'hello.sh' in the following manner, making sure to pipe the output through 'tr' in order to replace all the lowercase letters with those in the uppercase.

```
$yourname=$1

echo "Hello $yourname" | tr '[[:lower:]]' '[[:upper:]]'
```

Now if you have a desire to be concise, you may find that '$yourname' variable is not really necessary. The code will be simplified like so:

```
echo "Hello $1" | tr '[[:lower:]]' '[[:upper:]]'
```

Now slow down my friend. If you are able to create a script, you can execute like so:

```
bash hello.sh
```

...then congratulations, you've learned an important concept. You've just learned how programmers stuff complicated things into a 'container' that can be run into one line. Before we start making some decisions, let's see how we can use a feature known as variables to refer to data, which includes commands' output or results.

Bash Variables And Command Substitution

Variables are symbolic names for chunks of memory to which values can be assigned and its contents read and manipulated. At the very least, these 'symbolic names' helps make code more readable to us.

Nonetheless, variables essentially become more practical or useable in more advanced programming where you'll find situations where the actual values are not known- that is, before a program is executed. A variable is therefore more like a placeholder that is solved upon the actual execution time.

Let's take an example:

Assume 'websites. txt' has a list of website addresses. The routine below reads every line (through 'cat' which is really not best practice- but it will do for now) into a 'for loop', which in turn downloads all the URLs (please find details about for loops in the next chapter).

```
for url in $(cat websites.txt); do
  curl $url > megapage.html
done
```

Before you start getting confused, let me take you through a little introduction of the basic usage and syntax of variables.

Setting A Variable

The command below assigns 'Hello world' to 'var_a' variable and '42' to 'another_var'

```
user@host:~$ var_a="Hello World"
```

```
user@host:~$ another_var=42
```

Unlike most languages that you'll find today, bash is quite picky about the variable setting syntax. More specifically, it doesn't allow any whitespace between the name of the variable, the equal sign and the value.

These three examples would easily trigger an error from Bash:

```
var_a= "Hello World"
```

```
var_a = "Hello World"
```

```
var_a ="Hello World"
```

Referencing The Variable's Value

Sometimes, that is referred to as parameter substitution or expanding the variable.

```
user@host:~$ var_a="Hello World"
user@host:~$ another_var=42
user@host:~$ echo $var_a
Hello World
user@host:~$ echo $another_var
42
user@host:~$ echo $var_a$another_var
Hello World42
```

When De-Referencing Is Not Done

In the instance the sign '$' is not preceding the name of a variable, or the variable reference is inside single quotes, bash interprets the string literally like so:

```
user@host:~$ var_a="Hello World"
user@host:~$ another_var=42
user@host:~$ echo var_a
var_a
user@host:~$ echo '$another_var'
$another_var
user@host:~$ echo "$var_a$another_var"
Hello World42
user@host:~$ echo '$var_a$another_var'
$var_a$another_var
```

Concatenating Strings

You will find variables very useful when it comes to text-patterns that you'll use repeatedly:

```
user@host:~$ wh_domain='http://www.whitehouse.gov'
user@host:~$ wh_path='/briefing-room/press-briefings?page=
user@host:~$ wh_base_url="$wh_domain$wh_path"
user@host:~$ curl -so 10.html "$wh_base_url=10"
user@host:~$ curl -so 20.html "$wh_base_url=20"
user@host:~$ curl -so 30.html "$wh_base_url=30"
```

If the name of your variable is butting up against some literal alphanumeric character, this verbose form that involves curly braces will come in handy to reference the value of a variable:

```
user@host:~$ BASE_BOT='R2'
user@host:~$ echo "$BASE_BOTD2"
# nothing gets printed, because $BASE_BOTD2 is interpreted
# as a variable named BASE_BOTD2, which has not been set
user@host:~$ echo "${BASE_BOT}D2"
R2D2
```

The Valid Names For Variables

A variable name can have underscores and a sequence of alphanumeric characters. All the variables you create, as the user should begin with either an underscore or an alphabetical letter; not a number.

Here are some valid names for variables:

hey

x9

GRATUITOUSLY_LONG_NAME

_secret

When you write functions and scripts, in which arguments are passed in for processing, the arguments will automatically be passed 'int' variables named numerically- for instance, $2 and $3. A good example would be:

bash my_script.sh Hello 42 World

Commands will use $1 within 'my_script . sh' in reference of 'Hello', '$2' to '42' and '$3' for 'world'.

Take a look at the variable reference below:

'$0'

It will expand to the present name of the script- for instance, 'my_script . sh

What To Do Next With Linux?

We will continue to navigate the Ubuntu distro as we outline how to install and set up your operating system. Remember that one of the assets of any Linux OS is that you can customize it to work for you.

Desktop Version

With the Desktop version you will mostly find that most of it is plug and play. Graphics and text will guide you. Apps will allow you to navigate the functions that you need to do and to have, just as with Windows or MAC OS. Again, you will see icons, taskbars and menus that look familiar.

Graphics and CLI?

As mentioned earlier, although you are relying on the desktop version to provide a GUI, you will still have the ability to use the Command Line Interface (CLI) whenever you would like to do this. Different distros of Linux will have different ways of getting to these prompts. With Ubuntu in its various versions it may be some arrangement of clicking the Applications Menu, Accessories and finally the Terminal which is where you can get the prompt to enter the Commands.

You may feel that you chose the GUI edition to get away from having to use a CLI at all. Some people really like having this combination of graphics and the prompt however. Any future tutorials that you may watch or read may include some Commands that you may use at the prompts even with the desktop version. They may still apply to you. Some things to note about this are that it can be very useful to do things such as to automate tasks if you do the same things, often. It can also be very handy in times such as when your GUI crashes. It would be good to learn some of the basics, as you never know when you may need them!

Applications and Software

Upon installation, your Ubuntu distro already comes with many preinstalled apps and programs. These may include: Firefox, OpenOffice, music and video players, social media and messaging tools, and some of the usual apps that help make things useful or fun.

The best part about Linux is the customization. You should do a Google search for the best app, program or software for your needs if you are not sure what you should install, but the beauty is that you can customize, unlike preloaded systems with a lot of third party or proprietary stuff that most of us are used to having. Many of these come from repositories. Linux Repositories are places that house many programs and Apps that you can tap into at any time. Most of these are also open source. Some may not be.

With Ubuntu you will access news apps and software easily and at the touch of a mouse, quickly retrieve and install whatever you need.

Fetching New Apps (**www.webupd8.org**).

One quick and easy way to access the repositories is through what is called the Synaptic Package Manager. With this you can access games to MS Office. To into your System file, then under Administration click on the Synaptic Package Manager. Look for "ubuntu-restricted-extras" and install that through the package manager. This will allow access to some proprietary applications. In general, from this manager you can check what app you would like and install.

Another way to access the repository on the desktop version is to use the CLI Command. This will be outlined more in the Server section, where the CLI is essential, with the lack of the GUI. You will use Commands such as "apt-get-install" to fetch applications from the same repositories, but this will be text based through the CLI interface. Again, there are lists at the end of the guide. You will see a beginner's basic Command list that will be extremely helpful for navigating the CLI, even at the Desktop level. You will also see a more comprehensive list that will aid a beginner as well as move you into some intermediary learning.

One of the beauties of the Desktop version is this versatility.

Security, Updates and Efficiency

Every Linux user or developer will advise you to do some very specific things before you go in and play or do too much at first installing your version of Ubuntu. Security and Stability are also key for maintaining your Linux and you will enjoy it for many years. Here is a top 10 list of things Linux users recommend to do after the install.

1. Immediately Install and Update the Ubuntu version (although this sounds unnecessary if it is your first time using the system). This should be done in the case that there have been updates by the developers to patch and repair anything since the version was made available.
2. Adjust settings, appearances, and behaviors to your needs.
3. Be sure to adjust any Privacy settings as well to make things more secure.
4. Adjust themes, wallpapers and menus to your liking. A Tweak Tool may help provide more options.

5. Install AppGrid and Synaptic Package Manager to help find and install things quickly.
6. Install GetDeb and PlayDeb repositories, and sources of updates of software Personal Package Archives (PPAs), and be sure to Enable Partner Repositories (to access licensed software).
7. Disable Ads.
8. Install any media codecs, audio players and drivers now.
9. Install free apps and programs such as Google Chrome, Skype, GIMP, Spotify, etc.
10. Set up messaging, social media accounts, and cloud connections.

Creating Multiple Workspaces for the Desktop

You can also use workspaces to really maximize your desktop Ubuntu, to get more out of it, and to multitask for fun or pleasure. Some versions won't prominently display these options but they can be enabled in different distros, in different ways. You should check your distro and do a web search for how to activate Workspaces with your version. It usually just takes a few clicks.

Depending on the version of Ubuntu for example, in each of the environments you will need to click to either: Enable or Manage Workspaces, Add Applets, or Add Pager Widget to use these. Soon, you will have multiple workspaces which can help with organizing and separating your activities, assuming you have more than one at any time this will be quite useful. You should try and activate them, and test them out.

Multiple Workspaces in Ubuntu Linux

CLI

You should also probably learn some basic Commands that you could use at the Prompts, just in case (and, yes, that has been suggested a few times already).There are lists of Commands in the last Chapter of this guide. You will find that if you go into Applications, the Accessories, then get to the Terminal you can access the CLI and you will see a prompt. This is where the Commands come into play. Some users really like having this additional way to customize what they would like the system to do, to automate things, to take shortcuts.

Additionally, if you move on to the Server version at some point in time, you will already have some appreciation and knowledge of the Commands, as well as a better understanding of the structure and location of the system files. As you will later read, everything in Linux is a file. They differ in structure from those of Windows for example. By using the GUI you will see this from one perspective. When you use the CLI you truly will better understand how the file trees and directories work with the hardware and software to make what is known as your operating system. This is also where Linux enthusiasts get the feeling of freedom that comes with not only the open sourcing of applications and other system resources, but the freedom and flexibility to truly have your computer actively work for you.

Getting   Around   in   the   Server   Version

Sometime will need to be spent with the Server version however. It is not as straightforward and there are some particulars that will be very useful to know prior to, and during, exploring Linux in this way. If you know DOS it will be just a matter of learning Commands and code. If you do not, you will have a decent sized learning curve ahead of you.

To begin, you will login to your new Server Version, with the information you have provided. You will see just DOS screen with prompts at the Shell. You will not see the Graphic User Interface (GUI) as you would with the Desktop Version. You will now need to use commands to go anywhere at all within this new operating system. You should set up a very secure password and root (user) name. Make sure to document this exactly as is. Punctuation will matter very much with Linux. Different spelling equates to something entirely different. You will see this reminder again.

The Root of Everything

The word Root, in Linux, has a few meanings. The Root User is the Administrator (as the User name **root**) for the computer, which is the lightest level user, with full privileges.

147

Root also is the highest level, or core, of anything in Linux. It also is the location where it is installed, the equivalent to C:/Home in Windows. It's the highest level of file so to speak. All in Linux is either a directory or a file inside the directory, all within the Root directory.

The Command "sudo" means "Super User Do". This signifies that you, the Root User (i.e., the Administrator), have full permission to access files and programs. In some distros you will need to use this to preface some Commands.

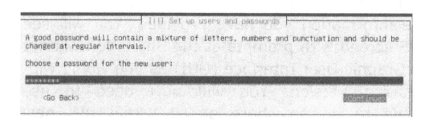

www.ubuntuserverguide.com

Get Command over Your Commands

As with most anything these days, you can do some simple research on Google to obtain large directories of Commands for Linux. And with these, you can navigate anywhere with Linux. The last Chapter of this book contains an extensive (but not exhaustive) glossary of Linux Commands. You should not expect to memorize this list, however you should begin to get familiar with the language of Linux.

Some of the most important and useful Commands will get you in, out, and around. To stress and expand upon an earlier point, your use of capitalization in Commands matters. Commands are very specific in their spelling so be careful to use proper capitalization. Spacing and word order also matter. You may not get anywhere, or you may end up somewhere that you did not intend to go.

In the long list of Commands and combinations of commands for Linux, there are also some "builtin" commands. Just as it sounds, Builtin commands are already contained within the Bash shell itself. When the first word of a simple command is a builtin, the shell carries out that command without requiring another program.

As said before, each distro will have its strengths and challenges. Something to note is that Commands for each distro may or may not be same. Given that the Commands are the only way to navigate this version of Linux, this is key. You should definitely have done some research not only on the distro that you have chosen, in regards to the compatibility and usage, but you also now want to research the specific Commands for that particular distro.

You will see there are some common roots to many of the Commands, and that you can build upon some with other Commands, keywords, file or program names. There are a few Commands that the beginner will need to use immediately. Follow along and try some out.

Get Help When You Need It

Here are a few simple things to know right off the bat. These may be your life jackets. "Man" pages are **manual (as in instructional) pages**. You will also, like the "sudo" Command, preface another Command with this Command. Using "man" opens up a screen with everything you need to know, as a digital **manual page**. Try these variations when in need. Knowing how to get somewhere, how to get out, and how to ask for help may seem very basic, but when you are learning the system these can be very frustrating.

"man –k"   To Search for all commands that involve a term. You may also use "apropos".

"man"   To Display help information.

"info"   To Display help information (differently).

"whatis"   To Display a description about a man page.

"whereis"   To tell the location of a man page.

To Exit a man page, you type "Q" (Quit), to drop out. This is the only way to back out of the   manual pages.

To Exit out of most other places, simply type "Exit".

The Commands "more" and "less" are also useful for displaying showing files that go past the screen you are on. You may need to read more information that what you can see on one screen on the help pages. This is especially important for a beginner on the system. Simply scroll down by using the space bar after typing the Command.

To get out, type in "q" for quit.

Moving around

You will soon learn that there are many directories in Linux, and you should get familiar with them. Although everything is a file Linux, a directory is a special type of file. Directories appear in lists, and related as a tree. Unlike OS that use GUI, you will not see the extension file names. Therefore you need to know how to navigate, find and change them. You should do a Google search for a list of them in order to properly navigate your system.

Just as with Commands, directory spelling and symbols also matter. As another note, the space bar comes handy when you need a legitimate space between letters and slashes, or letters from other words. It saves time and strokes. Missing these small details can also result in your being somewhere you don't need to or do not want to be. They can also dead end you with an error message. In worst case scenarios, mistakes in Linux could do some serious damage like deleting files. You should use underscore in lieu of spaces when setting up new file names. These small things will make a difference. A few directories and functions that beginners should become familiar with are:

/home- This is your root, file storage for documents and settings

/dev- Holds the device files

/cd- Change directory

/etc- This is similar to a control panel

Using directories

The Command "pwd" will print your working directory. This is also a good place to see where you are starting.

To see what is in the directories, beginning with your home directory, and any others thereafter, you can type "ls" to list what is in the directory.

Note that there are also hidden files that come with your home directory when the server account was configured. To see them listed, you must use a period character. For example, you would not just type "ls", but you would type "ls –b" to see the hidden files.

You will also learn to combine Commands as with the ones prior. For example, to move to a sub-folder named "xyz", you would preface the xyz as such, "cd xyz".

An example of the "cd" Command to navigate to your desktop directory,

type "cd ~/Desktop".

To return back to the root directory, type "cd~". An example of the same command used to navigate into the root directory is to type "cd /". To go to the parent directory, just before your current one), you should type "cd.."

You may want to explore some directories and try moving around to get your bearings before you proceed.

How to Install Programs

The Command "apt-get" gets and installs individual visual software packages. This is how you will create your server. You will manually pull in anything that you need to individualize your Linux server, using select Commands.

Repositories house many Linux programs that you can tap into at any time. These are also open source. You should do a Google search for the best software fit for your needs if you do not know what you need at this point.

To then access the Repository, for example, you would type "sudo apt-get install (program name)" to retrieve a copy to automatically install.

The Command "tasksel" means **task-select** with Ubuntu. If you run this, a screen will appear that gives you a list of common server type, packages and tasks. You can select and install whatever you need for your server.

For example, you would say "sudo apt-get install tasksel" to get the **tasksel** function, and then use it by using "sudo apt-get install (then the name of the task you want, server you want, etc.)".

If you wanted to install the LAMP server, you would type the command "sudo apt-get install lamp-server" to automate this.

```
daniel@office:~$ sudo apt-get install 64studio-apt
Reading package lists... Done
Building dependency tree
Reading state information... Done
The following NEW packages will be installed
  64studio-apt
0 upgraded, 1 newly installed, 0 to remove and 0 not upgraded.
Need to get 3,382B of archives.
After this operation, 45.1kB of additional disk space will be used.
WARNING: The following packages cannot be authenticated!
  64studio-apt
Install these packages without verification [y/N]? y
Get: 1 http://apt.64studio.com/backports/ lucid-backports/main 64studio-apt 0.1~lucid1 [3,382B]
Fetched 3,382B in 0s (8,376B/s)
Selecting previously deselected package 64studio-apt.
(Reading database ... 271609 files and directories currently installed.)
Unpacking 64studio-apt (from .../64studio-apt_0.1~lucid1_all.deb) ...
Setting up 64studio-apt (0.1~lucid1) ...
```

An example of an apt-get install (**www.en.flossmanuals.net**).

If you need help at any time, now that you know the man page Command, you would type: "man taskel". You would see man pages appear to address your need.

How to Uninstall

To uninstall, you would simply type "apt-get remove (and the name of the server in this case)". Use this Command for obtaining most of your software, and opting for the free, open source software to start.

Updates

After installation your software, you can use the upgrade command "sudo apt-get upgrade". Easy updates by way of the repository. It is easy to manually update them than to set automatic updates. You won't need them that often due to Linux efficiency. It is also more secure.

Task Manager: The "**top**" prompt command is similar to the "task manager" to see processes and how much space each is taking, or to stop things from running.

Use Command "**h**" for a list of Commands you may need at any time.

Enter the Command "**sudo top**" (to access the task manager, or the top), then the Command "**K**" (for kill) and then type the process ID number (called a PID) that you see next to the process that you want to kill.

Stop/Start/Restart Services

Linux servers need very infrequent rebooting, but at times when you may need to restart software or service.

To start/stop or restart you will type in the Command:

"sudo/etc/init.d/(name of program) start" : (**or stop or restart),** to make changes, and go offline while you work on the changes, such as with a crash, or reconfiguring files.

###

Now that you have some basic knowledge of where you are, where to go, how to get, install, or remove things, take some time to test these out. A list of Common Commands follows, as well as a more Comprehensive (but not exclusive) List. This is in no way exhaustive, but it does show some of the tasks that you may be able to do right now, or that you may look forward to learning.

Linux is an evolving OS, and given the diversity of distros and environments, things will only continue to change. As we advanced technologically, there are more and more opportunities to improve upon and to utilize Linux systems.

List of Top 35 Commands for Beginners-

If you have to memorize them

1. apt-get   Search for software packages and install
2. bzip2   Compress/decompress a file
3. cd   Change Directory
4. chmod   Change access permissions for a file
5. cp   Copy one or more files or directories location
6. date   Display or set the date & time
7. df   Display free and used disk space
8. emacs Text editor
9. exit   Exit shell
10. find   Search for files that meet a certain pattern
11. hostname Print or change system name
12. install Copy files, set/change attributes
13. locate   Search and find files
14. ls   List information about directory contents
15. man   Display help information for a certain command
16. mkdir   Create new folder/directory

17. mv   Move or rename directories and files
18. nano   Text editor with shortcuts to menus
19. open   Open a file in original application
20. ps   Display of current process status
21. pwd   Display/Print working directory
22. quota   Display disk use, limits
23. reboot Reboot system
24. rm   Remove, delete directories or files
25. rmdir   Remove, delete, empty directories or folders
26. shutdown Shutdown or restart
27. sftp   Secure File Transfer Program
28. sudo   Execute command as certain user with all permissions
29. tar   Store, list or extract files from a tarfile or tarball/archive
30. top   List resources and processes currently running
31. uptime Show uptime of system
32. wget   Retrieve a file or a web page(HTTP, HTTPS or FTP)
33. yum   Package manager to install from repositories
34. zip   Archive files
35. zip / unzip – Creates a .zip archive or extracts from a .zip archive

The easiest way to run Kali Linux is to run it "live" from a USB drive. The method also has a lot of advantages.

Advantages of a Bootable USB Drive

Non-destructive

It does not make any changes to your machine or your existing operating system on the machine as it runs directly from the USB drive. To go back to your existing setup without Kali Linux, you simply need to unplug the USB drive and restart your system.

Portability

You can carry the Kali Linux operating system on any USB drive in your pocket and have it running on any machine that is available to you.

Customizable

As discussed in the previous chapter, you can use scripts from the Kali Linux GitHub repository to build your custom Kali Linux installation ISO image and load it onto a USB drive as well.

Persistency

With a little bit of customization, you can make your Kali Linux Live USB drive store persistent data that will be retained across reboots.

Requirements to create a Kali Linux USB

1. A verified copy of the Kali Linux ISO to suit the system that you intend to run or install it on.

2. If you are using Windows, you will require the Win32 Disk Imager software to create the Kali Linux USB drive. On Linux or OS X, you can use the dd command on the terminal, which is pre-installed for creation of bootable USB drives.

3. A USB drive which has a capacity of 4GB or more. If your system supports an SD card slot, you can use an SD card as well with a similar process.

Installing

Let's go through the procedure of creating a USB drive for Kali Linux. The process will vary as per the host system on which you are creating the USB.

Windows

1. Plug the USB in a USB slot on your machine and note down which drive letter is designated to it. Launch the Win32 Disk Imager application that you had downloaded earlier.
2. Choose the ISO file for Kali Linux installation and ensure that you have selected the correct USB drive to be written it to. Click on Write.
3. Once the writing to the USB drive is complete, you can eject the drive and use it as a bootable USB drive to boot Kali Linux Live or install Kali Linux on your machine.

Linux

Creating a bootable USB drive is fairly simple in a Linux operating system. Once you have downloaded your Kali Linux ISO file and verified it, you can use the dd command on the terminal to write the file to your USB drive. You will need root or sudo privileges to run the dd command.

Warning: If you are unsure as to how to use the dd command, you may end up writing the Kali Linux image to a disk drive that you did not intend to. Therefore, it is important that you are alert while you are using the dd command.

Step One

You will need to know the device path to be used for writing the Kali Linux image to the USB drive. Without having the USB drive inserted in the USB slot, execute the following command in the command prompt in the terminal window.

sudo fdisk -l

You will get an output that shows you all the devices mounted on your system, which will show the partitions as

/dev/sda1

/dev/sda2

Step Two

Now, plugin the USB drive and run the same command "sudo fdisk -l" again. You will see an additional device this time, which is your USB drive. It will show up as something like

/dev/sdb

The size of your USB drive will be written against it.

Step Three

Proceed to write the image carefully on the USB drive using the command shown below. In the above example, we are assuming that the name of your Kali Linux ISO file is "kali-linux-2019.1-amd64.iso" and it is in your present working directory. The block size parameter bs can be increased, but the ideal value would be "bs=512k".

The writing to the USB drive will take a few minutes, and it is not abnormal for it to take a little more than 10 minutes to finish writing.

The dd command will not show any output until the process is completed. If your USB drive has an LED, you will see it blinking which is an indicator of the disk being written on. Once the dd command has been completed, the output would be something like this.

5823+1 records in

5823+1 records out

3053371392 bytes (3.1 GB) copied, 746.211 s, 4.1 MB/s

This will end the processing of the equations. You can now use the USB drive to boot into Kali Linux Live or start and installation of Kali Linux on a machine.

Creating a Bootable Kali USB Drive on OS X

Apple OS X is a UNIX based operating system. So creating a Kali Linux bootable USB drive on OS X is similar to that of creating on in Linux. After downloading and verifying your copy of the Kali Linux ISO, you can just use the dd command to write the ISO to your USB drive.

Warning: If you are unsure as to how to use the dd command, you may end up writing the Kali Linux image to a disk drive that you did not intend to. Therefore, it is extremely important to be alert while you are using the dd command.

You can use the following steps to write the ISO to your USB drive.

Step One

Without plugging in your USB drive to your MAC desktop or laptop, type the following command on the command prompt of the terminal window.

diskutil list

Step Two

A list of device paths showing all the disks mounted on your system will be displayed along with the data of the partition.

/dev/disk1

/dev/disk2

Step Three

Now plug in the USB and run the diskutil list command again. You will see that the list now shows your USB drive as well. It will be the one that did not show up for the first time. Let us assume that it is

/dev/disk6

Step Four

You can unmount the USB disk from the system using the following command:

/dev/disk6

diskutil unmount /dev/disk6

Step Five

Proceed further to carefully write the Kali Linux ISO on to your USB drive using the following command. This is assuming that your present working directory is the same as that in which your ISO file is saved. The block size parameter bs can be increased, but the ideal value would be "bs=1m".

The writing to the USB drive will take a few minutes, and it is not abnormal for it to take a little more than 10 minutes to finish writing.

The dd command will not show any output until the process is completed. If your USB drive has an LED, you will see it blinking which is an indicator of the disk being written on. Once the dd command has been completed, the output would be something like this.

That will be the end of the processing of the equation. You can now use the USB drive to boot into Kali Linux Live or start and installation of Kali Linux on a machine.

165

To boot from the desired drive on an OS X machine, press the "Option" button immediately after the computer powers on and select the drive you wish to use.

Installing and Setup

Once you are able to choose the distribution that you prefer, you can download or the installation package or get a Live CD distribution to get Linux into your computer.

Make space in your hard drive.

If you are going to install Linux in a PC computer, you may want to shrink the partition occupied by the Windows OS in order to make room for Linux. To do this, you will need to make a partition that your computer can boot from after the setup. This is applicable to distributions that need to be installed on the hard drive, such as Debian and Fedora.

You can create a partition using Windows, or you can simply boot the distro that you have and then use the partition editor GParted. This program is capable or repartitioning NTFS drives, which are typically used by later Windows versions.

Tip: If you are going to use a distribution that uses Live CD (such as Ubuntu), you will not need to create a partition for Linux. You can simply boot from the CD, and then the installers will perform the shrinking on your Windows partition.

Warning: There is a risk of losing all data when you partition your hard drive. Before you attempt to resize any drive partitions, see to it that you have already backed up all your files.

Using Live CD and Bootable USB distributions

Many Linux distros are capable of running from a thumb drive or a Live CD and do not require you to make the commitment of having to install them in your drive. This means that you can first try out their features and even save programs in these media. However, you may find that you need more space or you want the operation to be faster the next time you boot your computer on a Linux environment. If you think that you have the distro that you want, double-click on the icon that displays Install and follow the installation wizard.

The installation wizard will typically guide you through the following processes:

1. Preparation

This ensures that you are installing your Linux distro on a machine that meets its hardware requirements. You may also get asked if you want to include some third-party software, such as MP3 playback plugins, during this part of the installation.

2. Wireless setup

If you want to download updates or any third-party software, this part will walk you through setting up your wireless connection.

3. Hard drive allocation

This step will allow you to choose how you want Linux to be installed. You can choose to redo an installation of Linux, use dual booting and install Linux while another OS is in your computer, replace an existing OS with Linux, or upgrade a Linux distro that was previously installed.

4. Location

This sets up your computer's location on the map. This is essentially helpful when it comes to communicating with other Linux users and interacting with the Linux community.

5. Keyboard layout

This allows you to select the keyboard that you want to use for the OS

6. User setup

This allows you to select your username and password.

Conclusion

I hope that this book has helped you learn how to use Linux confidently, from installing it into your computer to creating your own programs using this operating system.

I also hope that this book has served as a guide in choosing the best Linux distribution for your needs, as well as applications that will help you perform daily computing tasks. By the end of this book, you should have also learned how to operate within Linux environment using the command line and have managed to learn some steps in making your system secure.

While not as popular as Windows—at least, for some—Linux is definitely one of the most reliable Operating Systems around—and the best part about it is that it's free, so you don't really have to pay for anything just to get it, and you also wouldn't have to go for counterfeit types of Operating Systems just because you could not pay for the legal copy.

The next step is to learn more about creating and editing shell scripts and create automation scripts that will allow you to use Linux in a more efficient manner.

LINUX
FOR BEGINNERS

A Beginners guide to

Linux Programming

Step-by-By-Step

Respective authors own all copyrights not held by the publisher.

The information herein is offered for informational purposes solely and is universal as such. The presentation of the information is without a contract or any type of guarantee assurance.

The trademarks that are used are without any consent, and the publication of the trademark is without permission or backing by the trademark owner. All trademarks and brands within this book are for clarifying purposes only and are owned by the owners themselves, not affiliated with this document.

Introduction

A Linux distribution is largely the sum of the things that you want to run Linux on your computer. There are numerous exclusive Linux distributions, each with their own target audience, set of functions, administrative tools, and fan club, the latter of which is extra well referred to as a consumer network. Placing apart the downright enthusiasts, most of the contributors of the consumer community for any Linux distribution are folks who simply occur to locate themselves the usage of a distribution for one motive or another. These reasons variety from what they've heard from buddies, what CD or DVD got here with a Linux magazine that they sold, to what Linux ebook they came about to shop for. Ubuntu Linux is the maximum exciting Linux distribution in years. Paradoxically, even as Ubuntu itself is indeed new, it additionally comes with a decent Linux pedigree. Ubuntu has direct roots in one of the oldest and greatknown Linux distributions available, the Debian GNU/Linux distribution. The folks that initially created and supported Ubuntu, Canonical Ltd., began out as Debian fans who desired a fastertransferring, greater updated distribution than Debian furnished. So, in the spirit of Linux and the Open source movement, they made their personal distribution, Ubuntu Linux, with the aid of incorporating the excellent of Debian, other Linux distributions and open source programs, and introduced their personal special sauce. Ubuntu approach "humanity to others." For the folks who use and produce you Ubuntu Linux, this is not just a name with touchyfeely overtones. The special sauce in Ubuntu is a social and enterprise devote ment to Ubuntu users everywhere. Ubuntu releases occur regularly, each six months, and support and updates for any Ubuntu launch are available for at the least eighteen months after that. Greater approximately that it within the first chapter, in which you'll read extra about Ubuntu, its philosophy, its network, and why the sum of these makes Ubuntu extraordinary than another Linux distribution.

In a nutshell, Ubuntu is a Linux distribution for human beings. At the same time as reading this e book, you'll see that there are lots of super technical motives for the usage of Ubuntu, even in case you're a toughcenter Linux propeller head. However, that's now not the point of ubuntuubuntu is for people who need to apply their computer systems and want a solid software basis for doing so. Whether or not your recognition is on writing code or browsing the net, sending and receiving e mail, working together with your virtual pix, watching dvds, lis tening to music, and so forth, Ubuntu offers the software program that you need to do what you need to do. Like any Linux distribution, you can freely down load and install Ubuntu, however it receives even better. This ebook consists of a CD of the today's Ubuntu computing device CD at the time this book become published, but new ver sions may be available by the point you purchase the ebook. If you don't have get entry to to a CD burner, need a ver sion of Ubuntu for a nonx86 system, or absolutely don't have the time, the Ubuntu folks will send you cds that you can both use to install or take a look atdrive Ubuntu in your cuttingedge computer system. That's more than looseit's revolutionary! Downloadable copies of Linux distributions are nothing new, but sending people physical cds in the event that they need them shows that Ubuntu Linux is extra than simply some other Linux distribution the Ubuntu parents are Linux devotees on a mission. And you and i are the fortunate winners.

Ubuntu Linux is a Linux distribution based in 2004 and centered on the needs of end users. Ubuntu Linux is the fabricated from the Ubuntu task subsidized by way of Canonical, Ltd. A enterprise based by way of Mark Shuttleworth, a a hit South African entrepreneur, long time Debian Linux developer, and preferred open source propose. Ubuntu is a Debianbased totally Linux distribution that makes use of a graphical person interface called GNOME as its computer surroundings. Sister projects to Ubuntu encompass Kubuntu, a model of Ubuntu that makes use of the KDE computing device environment instead of GNOME, Xubuntu, a model of Ubuntu that makes use of the lighterweight Xfce computer, and Edubuntu, a version of Ubuntu that makes a speciality of edu cational programs and popularizing using Linux in school. Everything has to have a name, however what is the Ubuntu in Ubuntu Linux? Now not too extraordinarily, the Ubuntu Linux internet website places it fine:

Ubuntu is an historical African phrase, which means "humanity to others." Ubuntu additionally method "I am what i'm because of who all of us are." The Ubuntu Linux distribution brings the spirit of Ubuntu to the software world.

Even though that may be a bit sensitive for a few, it's tough to argue with success and commitment. In 2005, its first year of availability, Ubuntu Linux acquired awards inclusive of the Linux journal's Reader's option award, Tux mag's Reader's preference 2005 for preferred Linux Distribution award, Ars Technica's excellent Distribution award, the United Kingdom Linux & Open source enterprise's best Distribution award, and the Linux international Expo's quality Debian byproduct Distribution award. No longer too shabby for the brand new distribution at the block. Aside from its technical excellence and value (and a few top investment way to Mark Shuttleworth), lots of the achievement up to now of Ubuntu Linux is due to the truth that its creators and proponents are not just the conventional Linux fanatics, but are without a doubt dedicated to growing and promoting a usable and without difficulty managed Linux distribution for give up consumers all over the global.

Chapter 1

1.1 Ubuntu Linux Project

Personal computers and their working structures have come an extended manner because the overdue Seventies, while the first domestic laptop hit the market. At that point, you may simply toggle in a program with the aid of flipping switches on the front of the machine, and the device ought to then run that application and best that application till you manually loaded any other, at which era the primary application became kicked off the device. Today's private computers offer powerful graphics and a rich consumer interface that makes it easy to pick and run a huge form of software program simultaneously. The primary domestic computer customers had been a network of interested folks that just desired to do something with these early machines. They fashioned pc golf equipment and published newsletters to share their pursuits and knowhow and often the software that they wrote for and used on their machines. Sensing opportunities and a developing marketplace, lots of computer companies sprang up to write down and promote specific programs for the laptop structures of the day. This software ranged from packages along with phrase processors, spreadsheets, and games to running systems that made it simpler to manage, load, and execute distinct applications.

Although the strength and capabilities of nowadays personal computer systems is midyears past the competencies of those early machines, the idea of writing software and freely sharing it with others in no way went away. Even though it by no means were given a good deal press because no one changed into making a living from it, unfastened software (and frequently its supply code) has persevered to be available from computer golf equipment, bulletin boards systems, and pc networks together with these days' net. The loose software program movement ultimately blossomed with three seminal occasions:

- The introduction of the GNU project by using Richard Stallman in 1983, a task dedicated to developing software whose source code would continually be freely available.

- The announcement of the loose software foundation (FSF) first of all devoted to fundraising for the GNU project.

- The creation of a free operating system task in 1991 that came to be known as Linux, by using a Finnish computer software program pupil named Linus Torvalds.

The working machine and programs mentioned on this e book are free, and their source code is freely available.

All of us who wants to can construct, set up, and run them. A massive online network of customers has sprung up around them, including specialized companies who create without problems established sets of this software, known as Linux distributions. This chapter explores the philosophy, community, and history at the back of one of the latest, and arguably the great, of those easily acquired, without problems set up, and easy to use free software program environments, known as the Ubuntu Linux distribution.

1.2 Linux Distribution

If you've been curious about Linux for some time, you are likely to notice that a bewildering range of versions of it seem to be available. Pc magazines and Linux related websites speak pink Hat Linux, SUSE Linux, the Novell Linux laptop, Fedora center Linux, and plenty of different matters finishing in Linux, each to be had from a specific enterprise or enterprise. Understanding precisely what humans mean while they are saying "Linux" is the key to information how such a lot of exclusive variations of the same component can be available, however that requires a little perception into how private computers in reality work from the software program factor of view.

When you set up a running device such as Linux, Microsoft home windows, or Apple's Mac OS X on your laptop system, you're installing a few amount of software that is invisible to any ordinary person because it runs behind the curtain. This software program handles scheduling, beginning, and stopping unique packages, communicating together with your laptop's hardware, dealing with communications with peripherals consisting of your printer, and so forth. This is usually referred to as machine software due to the fact normal users don't at once interact with it, but it wishes to be present and going for walks to offer the services that application software is predicated on. The core piece of this device software is usually known as a kernel due to the fact it is the valuable piece of the working device and the entirety else builds upon the fundamental services that it offers. By way of itself, a kernel isn't very interesting humans don't definitely want to run a kernel, they need to run applications. These applications depend upon services which can be provided each by way of the kernel and through another machine software program. For instance, if you want to print a record, anything application you're the use of desires to create a version of your report this is formatted in a manner that your printer is aware, and then timetable that file for printing. Some other piece of software program handles sending the formatted file to the printer, ensuring that the File prints successfully, and so on.

In famous usage, "Linux" is the collective name for a running system kernel and its associated applications. In reality, Linux is technically the name of just the kernel most of the applications that all and sundry uses with Linux come from other unfastened software tasks. A Linux distribution is the precise term for a Linux kernel, a hard and fast of programs which can run on top of it (irrespective of in which they arrive from), and a tool to put in every aspect and configure your system. Each company or company that offers a Linux distribution is taking gain of the opensource nature of the Linux kernel and the packages that run on top of it through setting together the "right" version of the Linux kernel with what they view as the "right" collection of middle applications that anyone would need to run on top of it.

Chapter 2

2.1 Installations

Here are various ways to install Ubuntu:

1. You can dual boot Ubuntu with Windows (so that you can have the authority to use both operating systems at a time of your choosing)
2. You can install Ubuntu inside a virtual box in Windows
3. You can use Bash on Windows feature to install it inside Windows
4. You can even solely install Ubuntu by wiping windows entirely out of your system.

Installation of ubuntu by replacing windows or other operating system out of the system

What do you really need in order to install Ubuntu:

- A USB of at least 4 GB in size. You can use a DVD too.
- Net connection (for downloading Ubuntu and liveusb making device, no longer required for putting in Ubuntu)
- Optionally, you can want an external USB disk for making a backup of your important statistics (if any) present at the modern system.

In case you are going to install the default Ubuntu GNOME, the system necessities are:

188

- A machine with 2 ghz twin core processor or better
- 4 GB of RAM or more
- At least 25 GB of tough disk space

1. Download Ubuntu

Before you do something, you have to download Ubuntu. It's far to be had as a single ISO File of round 2 GB in size. An ISO file is largely an image of disc and you need to extract this ISO on a USB disk or DVD. You can download Ubuntu ISO from its website.

2. Create USB

Once you've got downloaded Ubuntu's ISO report, the following step is to create a live USB of Ubuntu. A live USB basically permits you in addition into Ubuntu from a USB pressure. You could test Ubuntu without even installing it in your device. The equal stay USB also permits you to put in Ubuntu. There are various free gear available for making a live USB of Ubuntu along with Etcher, Rufus, Unbooting, typical USB installer.

3. Boot from live USB

Plug to your live Ubuntu USB disk to the system. Now, you want to make certain that your machine boots from the USB disk in preference to the difficult disk. You can do this by using shifting the USB up within the boot order. Restart your system. When you see a logo of your computer manufacturer (Dell, Acer, Lenovo and so on), press F2 or F10 or F12 to get entry to the BIOS settings.

4. Install Ubuntu

Now you need to boot into the stay Ubuntu surroundings. You'll the grub display screen that gives you the option to both attempt Ubuntu without putting in or set up it right away. You can choose the primary alternative i.e., 'strive Ubuntu without putting in':

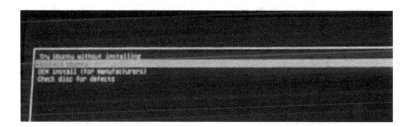

In around 1020 seconds, you ought to be capable of log in to the stay Ubuntu environment. It can take some more time in case you are using the slower USB 2.

Click on at the setup Ubuntu icon at the computer.

Choose your language

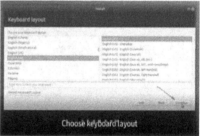
Choose keyboard layout

You must move for the normal installation right here because it will set up some software program like music participant, video players and a few games. In case you are related to internet, you'll get the option to download updates while installing Ubuntu. You could uncheck it due to the fact it is able to increase the installation time if you have a gradual net. You may update Ubuntu later as well with none issues.

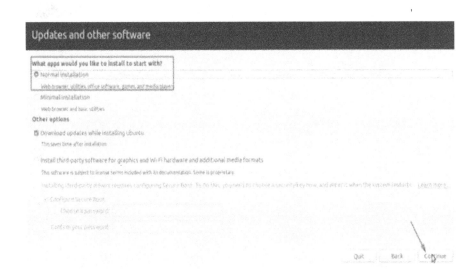

The maximum critical display comes at this time. If there are other operating systems hooked up, you could get the option to install Ubuntu along with them in dual boot. However, because your aim is to best have Ubuntu Linux on your complete machine, you have to cross for Erase disk and installation Ubuntu alternative.

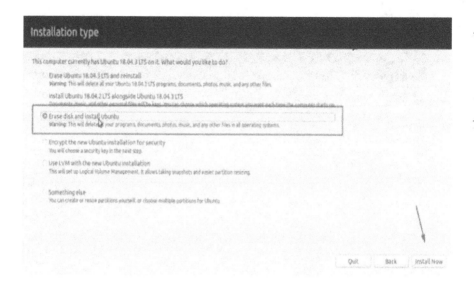

When you hit the "install Now" button, you'll see a caution that you are about to delete the information. You already know it, don't you?

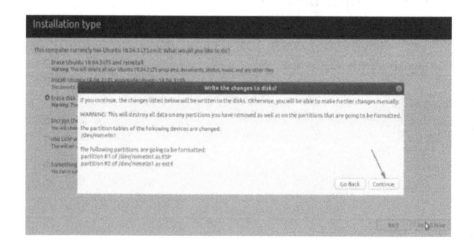

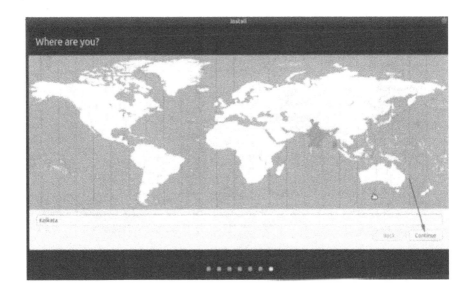

Create username, computers name or hostname and set the password.

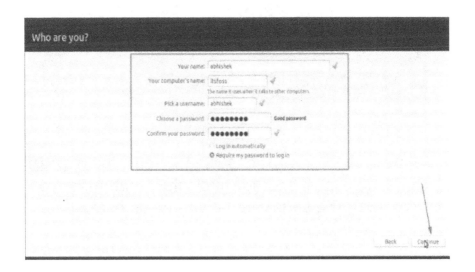

195

 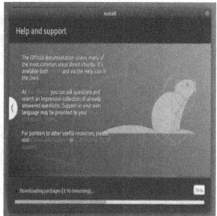

Once this process is finished you will be asked to restart the system.

While you restart the system, you would possibly come across a shutdown display that asks you to take away the setup media and press enter.

Remove the USB disk and press enter. Your device will reboot and this time, you'll boot into Ubuntu.

Installing Program from Desktop CD

The Ubuntu desktop CD now not simplest provides a fantastic way to attempt out Ubuntu, however, additionally presents an amazing manner to try out some powerful and excellent opensource packages for your home windows device. In case you insert an i386 Ubuntu desktop CD into the CD force of a system that's strolling Microsoft windows, you'll see a dialog like that shown in figure 2.1.

This dialog enables you to put in any of the subsequent packages for your windows system:

197

- Mozilla Firefox is an internet browser that gives a popular and cozy opportunity to Microsoft's net Explorer on windows structures. The center abilities furnished with the aid of Firefox are easily prolonged the use of hundreds of plugins which might be freely to be had over the net.
- Mozilla Thunderbird is an email client (MUA) that offers a famous and comfortable mechanism for reading e mail from POP/POP3 and IMAP mail servers.
- Abiword is a famous word processor that is a part of the GNOME office suite and affords a loose, opensource opportunity to expensive, proprietary word processors including Microsoft phrase.
- Gaim is an opensource alternative to maximum immediate messenger software which can trade messages in all the formats utilized by popular instantaneous messaging applications from AOL, Yahoo, and so on.
- GIMP is a popular image creation and manipulation bundle that gives a loose, open supply alternative to expensive, proprietary software program applications such as Adobe Photoshop.

As soon as the installation completes, these opensource applications run natively to your home windows device, without the need for the Ubuntu laptop CD. For instance, figure 2.2 indicates Firefox running natively on my home windows machine.

Figure 2.1

Opensource software for windows on Ubuntu CD.

Figure 2.2

Installing Firefox on windows from Ubuntu CD.

Figure 2.3

Running it.

Installation on Special Purpose System

The Ubuntu laptop CD's graphical installer differs from the quasigraphical, Debian based installers used on the Server and trade installation cds. Before providing a graphical installer at the desktop CD, Ubuntu's Debian based totally installer received its share of the complaint traditionally aimed at the Debian installer "It's no longer fancy enough," "It looks like something from 1985," "It doesn't use all the whizzy features of my 5dimensional, extended portraits card," and so on. Those are all genuine, and for properly motives. Although it's nice to have an elaborate, mouse orientated, graphical installation program, an installer is something which you use once in keeping with system after which neglect about. An installer therefore has to be rock stable, clean to underneath stand. It additionally has to paintings on any computer device from the maximum wretched, low decision VGA system to the excessive give up gaming structures of nowadays, which provide beautiful resolution and visible nuances that many human beings can't even discover. Server systems frequently run headless (i.e., without a graphical console), and therefore an installer that works on those types of structures in all fairness important.

Dual Boot System

Dual booting is the time period used to explain a computer system that could run a couple of running system (even though not at the identical time). Dual booting is an attractive option if you need to test with Ubuntu but nevertheless rely upon packages that run on whatever existing operating machine you're the use of. Because Ubuntu Linux is formally supported on x86 and 64bit pc machines that often run Microsoft windows and on personal computer systems that commonly run Mac OS X, this bankruptcy explains a way to install Ubuntu as a 2nd running device on those types of machines. The handiest requirement for doing that is that you have sufficient area for your pc's drives to maintain both operating systems and their associated programs.

2.2 Computer Boot Process

To apprehend how dual booting works, it's beneficial to have a touch perception into what precisely happens when you switch on a computer machine, that is known as your laptop's boot manner. When you turn to your laptop system, a hardware subsystem known as the fundamental enter Output system (BIOS) masses, explores and assessments your hardware, and then reads some configuration placing from a unique reminiscence chip on your system. On x86 systems, these BIOS settings specify a ramification of configuration facts inclusive of the order in which your hard force, CDROM, DVD, or different media are searched to discover something that it can execute. (On Apple Macintosh systems, that is robotically a disk partition until you genuinely specify an alternate boot device with the aid of preserving down a related key to your keyboard.) Once your machine knows wherein to boot from, it searches those devices and masses a grasp boot report from the bootable device. At this point, your system doesn't realize something approximately the geometry of your tough disks or different garage systems, however it can usually discover the primary few blocks on any device to identify whether or not the pressure is bootable. On Ubuntu Linux structures, the MBR carries the primary degree of the Linux GRUB boot loader, that's loaded into memory and is performed. The primary stage of the GRUB boot loader then loads a second degree of installer that knows the type of filesystem used at the bootable drive.

Once the second one level boot loader is loaded into reminiscence and executing, it reads a configuration record placed at the tool that contained the boot loader and shows any available alternatives for booting the computer system. On laptop systems that run best one working system, your boot alternatives are pretty straightforward, definitely listing one of its kind ways of starting that single working system. On systems that can boot multiple working systems, the boot loader alternatives list all the to be had operating systems on your laptop. Similarly, to providing multiple approaches of booting every working system, they generally also allow you to select between running structures. Loading a series of more and more complicated programs, starting with the BIOS or boot monitor and finishing with a blown operating device is known as booting your system due to the fact the system has basically pulled itself up by using its bootstraps.

2.2.1 Dual Booting System Configuration

It's quite easy to configure your system to run your desire of working structures. This enables you as well Microsoft windows or Mac OS X whilst you want to study mail from programs that best run under the ones running systems, but boot Linux when you need to do extra complicated tasks or want to discover the power and elegance of Ubuntu. Putting in a dual boot system is also an incredible manner to research Linux when you have only one laptop or computer and aren't inclined or capable of genuinely make the leap and flow to Linux fulltime. Whilst you installation Mac OS X or Microsoft windows on a system with a single disk power, these working systems usually create handiest a single partition on every of your disk drives. This makes it elaborate to add every other operating machine to that identical pc device. You usually have picks:

- Add any other tough power to that laptop machine and installation Linux there.
- Exchange the existing walls for your pc's hard power to free up area wherein you could
  Create every other partition where you may then set up Linux.

The primary of these is normally an option in computer systems, assuming that you have room inside your system for any other power, have sufficient funds to shop for some other disk pressure, and are devoted and technical sufficient to open up your pc and add a tough power efficaciously. However, if you have sufficient free space available on your device's existing drive, the second option is less expensive, quicker, and simpler. This bankruptcy specializes in putting in a machine with a current operating system putting in onto a second disk is equal to putting in on a single disk machine besides which you need to ensure that you pick the correct disk to install onto. As stated in advance on this bankruptcy, you ought to plan on devoting at the least 3GB to an Ubuntu Linux installation, which offers you sufficient area in which to put in the operating machine, a known set of packages, and enough room to create and save a reasonable amount of your Files and different personal records. 3GB does no longer leave you all that tons free space, however, is usable anything large than 3GB is, of course, better because it will provide extra area with the intention to create and save private facts and Files to your Ubuntu Linux partition. Converting the prevailing partitions for your computer device is called repartitioning your system.

Repartitioning Existing Disk

After you've achieved backups of your crucial files and proven that the backups are readable, you could flow on to certainly repartitioning your disk to make room for Linux. Step one in doing that is to defragment your disk, which packs the disk area associated with all of the Files and directories on your current partition as carefully together as feasible. Disks end up fragmented as you create and delete files there's nothing that you may do about it besides to clean things up every so often. When you repartition your disk, you're essentially reducing off a part of an existing partition so you can use it for something else. You can't simply cast off a part of a present partition if it carries elements of Files that you are the use of.

Defragmenting Windows

Windows provides a built-in defragmentation utility, which you could start via deciding on the applications ⇨ addons ⇨ device tools ⇨ Disk Defragmenter menu item. In this application, (proven in figure 2.4) first choose the drive letter associated with the disk partition which you need to reduce in length to make room for Linux, and then click Defragment. The Disk Defragmenter will do its work and display an earlier than and after photo of fragmentation on that partition once it completes. Strolling the Defragmenter as soon as is sufficient, despite the fact that the Defragmenter reviews that your disk continues to be incredibly fragmented.

You may marvel why figure 2.4 indicates some system Files that haven't been moved closer to the start of the disk. The defragmenter doesn't relocate Microsoft home windows system Files along with its paging report because those Files are used internally by using home windows and shouldn't be changed after they are created. However, they are recreated if any issues are located with them, so they'll be recreated although they're positioned in a part of the disk which you're going to allocate for use via Linux.

Figure 2.4

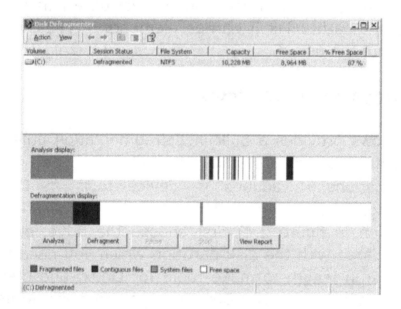

2.3 Defragmenting Mac OS Systems

Apple's Disk software is an exceptional tool for trying out the inner consistency of your Mac OS X HFS and HFS+ partitions. Unfortunately, it does no longer defragment disk partitions, so third party utilities are your only alternative while defragmenting or in any other case modifying Mac OS X disk walls. Mac OS X systems running Mac OS X 10.3 (Panther) and later that use the HFS+ journaling filesystem robotically defragment Files less than 20MB in size on every occasion these Files are up to date. Mac OS X 10.3 and more HFS+ filesystems also use a mechanism known as warm File Adaptive Clustering to position frequently used Files much less than 10MB in size in a unique portion of the filesystem, referred to as the hot band, that offers optimal overall performance primarily based on the characteristics of your disk pressure. Files moved to this place are defragmented as they're moved. Though it can provide substantial overall performance improvements, the usage of warm File Adaptive Clustering complicates life for defragmentation utilities. However, this is every other scenario where it's better to be secure than sorry. For PPC based Mac OS X structures, disk utilities inclusive of Micro mat's tech tool pro (my nonpublic preferred, to be had at www.micromat.com) perform defragmentation all through disk optimization

Figure 2.5

GNOME Partition

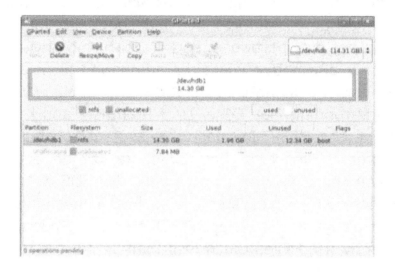

Chapter 3

3.1 Basic Linux Concepts

This chapter explains basic Linux system standards, that specialize in how records is stored and organized on all Linux systems and the way the Linux operating machine controls Access that information and to privileged operations. Other than specific sections on how Ubuntu offers with and grants high degree permissions, the statistic in this bankruptcy applies to any I inux device and to most other UNIX-like systems.

Working with Files and Directories

A File is nothing more than a set of data that programs, and your operating system can discover and cope with as a single unit. Files are containers for some type of records, whether they contain a letter in your mom or parole board, a duplicate of one in every of your favorite songs (legitimate, of direction), a virtual picture, or the information utilized by a spreadsheet to calculate the fitness of your private budget. Presenting the general idea of a file as a field for associated data makes it smooth for packages and Linux to discover and use that statistics. Hence the file menu that is present in maximum graphical programs today this menu consists of the commands that you use to open existing files, create new ones, and keep adjustments that you have made to any File which you are running with. Files are mandatory on a computer system the running machine has to have a manner to identify and Access statistics, the programs that it desires to run, any configuration Files used by the ones packages, and so on. In addition, whilst you turn it on, your laptop system needs to realize how to discover the working machine and related configuration facts that it calls for in addition. But, as increasingly Files had been required, used for kind of purposes and created by using extraordinary users, it didn't take lengthy for customers to look for an intermediate mechanism for organizing files, which brought about the advent of directories. Directories are truly packing containers for groups of related Files, and that they can also comprise directories (or subdirectories). That is what is called a hierarchical series of files the region of any unique report is described by means of identifying the series of directories that eventually comprise the record which you're looking for. The listing that everyone searches begin with on Linux structures is referred to as the foundation directory, due to the fact it is the place to begin for the outline of the way to navigate to any record this is saved regionally (i.e., in your pc). The same standard analogy for files and directories is a filing cabinet you can discover any file within the filing cupboard via following a manner like this: begin on the filing cupboard, open the first drawer, open the hanging record categorized personnel, pick the manila folder with your call on it, and test your healthcare enrollment shape. On a pc, the manner for finding the vicinity of an identical record might be something like this: visit the root of the filesystem (/), go to the home directory, visit the health listing (my login name), and search for the File named health_enrollment.txt.

Linux systems use the "/" character to split record and directory names, so this is frequently greater without a doubt expressed as, "get the record/domestic/health/health_enrollment.txt." The series of directories leading to a given file is regularly referred to as the "path" to that File.

Linux systems that provide a graphical user interface, including GNOME, provide graphical approaches of navigating via directories, commonly through clicking on them to open them and opening a window that shows graphical icons similar to the files that they incorporate. "using command line tools," any Linux command line surroundings makes use of a command known as cd (which stands for exchange listing) to navigate through a series of directories. You could exchange to every listing in a sequence of directories (paths) separately, or you could virtually cd to a specific target directory. In other phrases, the subsequent sequences of commands are equivalent:

Cd /

Cd home

Cd health

And

Cd /home/health

3.2 Linux Directory (Standard)

All Linux system offer a standard set of core directories. The subsequent directories are used to preserve programs that ought to run while you are booting your Linux device, configuration documents for those applications, libraries utilized by those packages, temporary files created via running packages, and so on:

- /: because the top degree listing of a Linux system, this directory need to exist in order that other directories may be positioned inside it.
- /bin: A listing that holds middle or core applications used by a Linux device.
- /dev: A listing that holds unique documents, called device nodes, which are used to access any devices that are connected to your Linux system.
- /etc.: A listing that holds system configuration information, carries the files that explain the collection of applications that execute on a Linux machine as a part of its boot manner, and save or store configuration documents for a number of the packages that are done with the aid of a Linux system.
- /lib: A directory that holds libraries of functions that may be known as with the aid of different applications.
- /proc: A listing wherein the Linux kernel tracks energetic tactics and standard status Data.

- /sbin: A directory containing applications which are generally finished best by the superuser.
- N /sys: A directory in which the Linux kernel tracks the reputation of device hardware and associated hardware interfaces.
- /tmp: A directory that holds transient files created by way of various applications on a running system.

3.3 Common Linux Directories

Relying on the number of documents you've mounted in your system and its format; you will probably locate several other directories on any Linux system. A few other usually used directories on Linux systems are the subsequent:

- /home: A directory that holds the subdirectories wherein exceptional users store their documents. For instance, most (if now not all) of the files owned via the person "health" are stored within the /home/health listing (or subdirectories of that directory). The directories used by character users to keep in step personal files are referred to as their "home directories" this call led to consumer directories being saved in /home, no longer the opposite manner around. On older Unix and UNIX like structures, customers' home directories had been stored under /usr (as "slash user) however are actually created under /home to simplify system improvements.

- Opt: A directory usually used when installing third party software. This directory takes its call from the idea that it contains "noncompulsory" software which could fluctuate across extraordinary machines.
- Usr: A directory hierarchy that carries files intended to be utilized by everyday customers as they use a Linux machine. The listing /usr/bin incorporates packages that users may want to execute, /usr/lib incorporates libraries used by the ones packages, and so forth.
- /var: A directory that holds different directories with variable content material. As an instance, the directory /var/log carries log files for machine applications and events. Those log files are created even as a device is running and can develop very big over the years.

Disks, Partition, Mount Points

In geek language, which means without imposing a few business enterprise at the system used to keep your facts, your operating gadget might haven't any concept where to search for specific documents, directories, or something. To store statistics on a disk and get entry to that facts afterward, a disk must be organized in such a way that your operating device and associated programs can study, write, and interact with. This preparation generally includes steps:

a.   Dividing the disk into one or more sections that can be uniquely placed via the running device. Every segment of a disk is called a partition.

b.   Formatting the partitions, called "creating a filesystem," in such a manner that your operating machine can access every partition and create files and directories there.

Disk drives are partitioned for several reasons:

•   To lessen the quantity of time required to discover a particular piece of statistics at the power. It honestly takes much less time (and less location data) to find a specific piece of information in a smaller pool of records.

•   To restrict the number of records that may be misplaced or broken if a disk or partition turns into corrupted.

•   To speed up administrative operations which include defragmentation, consistency checking, and repair (whilst necessary).

•   To simplify administrative operations, which includes backups. It's less complicated to back up partitions in order to in shape on a single tape or different backup media, due to the fact no operator intervention is required (consisting of switching tapes). A couple of walls also permit you to put in gadget files and packages on distinct partitions than where you shop your user information. You may then back up the partition containing user facts especially often, without by accident backing up a tremendous amount of fantastically unchanging executables, gadget files, and so on.

3.4 Standard and Journaling: Local Filesystem

Local filesystems are filesystems that are positioned on storage devices which might be physically connected for your laptop. Get Access to data on local filesystems is therefore rapid because they may be without delay connected in your device. Alternatively, local filesystems are beneficial simplest in case you and any other users who need access to the data that they include can connect to the system on which they are placed. While you want access to records this is saved in a local filesystem, connecting to the system on which specific data is physically placed normally isn't a hassle in these days networked environments you may always open an SSH (secure Shell) or telnet connection to that system, so long as that unique machine is up and working efficaciously, of path.

Journaling filesystems improve machine restart time because a filesystem can continually be made consistent by using playing any pending transactions in opposition to the filesystem. Therefore, running the **fsck** software commonly consists, at maximum, of executing any pending changes which can be recorded in the filesystem log. Journaling filesystems also can improve universal filesystem overall performance because the filesystem doesn't have to wait until a report replace completes efficiently, as preferred filesystems do. Once changes are written to the log, ordinary filesystem operations can hold, and the filesystem may be updated asynchronously. Due to the fact the log is usually stored in unique, high performance part of the filesystem that makes use of a special layout; log updates can be appreciably quicker than updates to the real filesystem. Obviously, modifications to any file ought to be completed earlier than that document may be modified once more, so it is important to check whether there are pending updates to a record before editing it.

3.5 Network File System

Network filesystems are filesystems which can be stored on far off systems (typically referred to as file servers) and may be set up to your local system similar to a local filesystem. Networked filesystems offer users with the freedom to access their information from any device on which they are able to log in and which has access to those networked assets.

Network filesystems provide several benefits over nearby filesystems:

- They reduce the threat that the failure of a single machine will prevent you from having access to your data. Most networked filesystems enable you to log in on a couple of machines and get access to your information in exactly the equal way.
- They offer central locations for information that need to or ought to be shared amongst all users.
- They simplify getting access to existing records from quicker systems. Think that you have written an application to check CPU and memory performance, or that your work or studies relies upon on CPU and memory in depth calculations. Strolling your software on a faster, greater powerful system is as simple as logging in on that system and walking the software from the networked filesystem.
- They provide the possibility to centralize administrative operations together with backups.
- They sell interoperability and versatility. You could commonly access networked filesystems from structures going for walks Linux, Microsoft home windows, Mac OS X, and so forth. This makes it easy in an effort to use the software

program and hardware that is great desirable in your desktop necessities and still access the same statistics at the networked filesystem.

Chapter 4

4.1 Linux Permissions

If you are sharing your Ubuntu device with different users, it is compulsory to understand how Linux structures protect files and directories in order that they can be accessed through handiest the people which you want to have access to them. Similarly, if you have established your own Ubuntu device and are therefore responsible for taking care of It ("device management" in geek language), you need to recognize how Ubuntu structures ensure that simplest unique, authorized users can perform privileged duties. As an instance, it'd be probably inconvenient if random users ought to format disk drives, reconfigure your system connection to networks which include the internet, and so forth. Even though you'd wish that no one might do these varieties of things maliciously, it's easy sufficient to by chance click on ok while exploring gadget configuration programs, questioning possibly that this will clearly exit from the application.

Linux supports the traditional permission model utilized by all Unix like structures, users and businesses, with a few interesting twists that have been delivered to foster Ubuntu's dreams of usability and person friendliness. If you've used different Linux systems inside the past, it's clean enough to conform to doing things the Ubuntu way, and if you're new to Linux, you will find the Ubuntu model for privileged commands to be pretty clean to understand, configure, and use.

4.2 Users and Groups

All Linux structures offer basic administrative entities which can be used to decide who has access to what files and who can carry out particular, privileged operations. Every person who can log in on a Linux system does so thru a user account, which includes a call and password, and which has a selected domestic directory that contains that user's configuration statistics in addition to any files that they devise. The document /etc /passwd (known as the password file, but why kind some more letters if you don't have to) incorporates a list of every person who has an account on that unique system.

All Linux users belong to one or more groups. A collection is an administrative entity that makes it less complicated for multiple users to get access to the same sets of files. Statistics about the corporations which are described to your Ubuntu machine and the customers that belong to those businesses is saved inside the file / etc /group, that is a text record with easy to apprehend entries. As explained later in this segment, file and directory permissions may be set such that customers who're a member of a distinctive organization can read and/or write files in shared directories, which other users at the machine nevertheless can't get admission to. This makes it easy to set up collaborative tasks or to absolutely percentage facts with decided on different customers to your structures.

4.3 File and Directory Permission in Linux

This section offers an overview of how file and directory permissions are displayed and used on Linux systems. It makes sense to introduce this topic here to demonstrate how user and group identities can provide shared access to files, directories, and other assets, and how to manage those settings. The very best command to use to view the permissions on a record or directory is the Linux ls (list) command, which shows information approximately the files and directories in a specific area. As an instance, the command ls ld /home/health presents a protracted list of my home listing, which includes data about the contemporary permissions on that directory:

drwr-xr-x   144   health   7727   20210705   11:35 /home/health

The permissions field of ls output can be broken down into four sections:

The first man or woman, which identifies the kind of item you're looking at. The maximum commonplace of those are a if the factor you're listing is a normal file, a d if it's a directory, a c if it's a device node that may be accessed as a move of characters, or a b if it's a tool node that can be accessed as a block tool.

Three sets of three characters, which constitute the permissions that the owner, the group owner, and all others have on the document or listing.

The most common values for each function inside the 3 permissions sections are r, which means that that the record or directory may be study, a w, this means that that the report or listing can be written to, and an x, which (for a file) method that the file may be performed or (for a listing) means that the directory can be searched for other files or directories. If any of these permissions are not set, its position is represented by way of a dash. Further, the user and organization execution bits can be set to an s, which means that "set person or organization identification upon execution" in different words, executing that record is done as even though it were being performed by using the owner and/or institution of the specified document. This is normally carried out to execute a command as even though it had been being performed by using any other, greater privileged user to your device.

4.4 Default Permissions

A umask is the classic Unix mechanism for placing the default protections of document and directories which you create. By means of default, the umask is a four digits of octal variety that is logically and with the customary file protections of octal 0666 (ironically) whilst you create a record or octal 0777 whilst you create a listing. The default umask fee on maximum Linux distributions is 0002, that means that any report you create is created with the octal safety mode 0664 both the owner and group can examine and write any report that you create, however random can handily read the record. Similarly, any listing that you create is created with the octal safety mode 0775 both the proprietor and organization can create files in that directory, and all of us can listing the contents of the directory and search for documents in it. You discover a person's default umask setting through issuing the umask com mand from any Linux command line prompt. Most of the people set their umask to 0022 in their shell configuration command record (generally ~/.bashrc) to change their default record introduction settings so that files can most effective be written through their owners (i.e., are created with an octal protection of 0644) and directories can simplest been written to by using their owners (i.e., are created with an octal safety of 0755). The capability to define a umask is built into all Unix shells; for greater information about placing or the use of your umask, see the online documentation for the shell that you are the use of (commonly the bash shell, as mentioned in bankruptcy 6, "the usage of Command Line equipment").

4.5 Privileged Operations in Ubuntu

Aside from your own person call and numeric identification, the maximum vital other person call on a Linux device is the user named root, whose user identification and group id are each 0, and who's frequently known as the superuser.

On most Linux systems, privileged operations are often done by using the use of the su (substitute user ID) command to turn out to be the basis person. However, Ubuntu does things slightly in another way. Ubuntu uses the sudo (alternative consumer id do) command to perform all privileged operations. The sudo command makes use of the text layout configuration file /and so on/sudoers to determine which customers can carry out privileged operations as the superuser. On Ubuntu systems, any member of the admin group can carry out privileged operations as the basis consumer. You could use the sudo command on any Linux system, however you cannot use the su command on an Ubuntu machine.

The difference among the usage of the su and sudo commands is diffused but great:

- When the use of the su command to carry out a privileged operation, you execute the su command, supply the basis consumer's password in response to the password set off, which then begins a subshell with root privileges. You then execute whatever privileged instructions you need within the con textual content of that shell. They may be all therefore finished because the superuser. When you are done, you can both exit from that shell or suspend it for next reuse.
- While using the sudo command, you execute the sudo command, accompanied by using the call and arguments to the command which you want to execute.

Chapter 5

5.1 GNOME Desktop

Even though many curmudgeons and longtime Unix customers eschew any type of graphical interface, allows face it the majority nowadays want (and anticipate) one. The graphical environment used on Ubuntu structures, the GNOME laptop, affords a stable and usable environment for strolling your graphical applications and interacting with your device graphically. Most of the Linux utilities used for device administration and configuration provide graphical interfaces to simplify formerly complicated tasks and are without problems accessed from one of the primary menus provided through the GNOME computer.

5.1.1 GNOME Desktop Overview

Figure 5.1 shows the default GNOME laptop on an Ubuntu Linux system the primary time you log in. This figure also presentations a single utility window for instance you won't see that except you explicitly pick the packages ⇨ accessories ⇨ Terminal menu command, but I desired if you want to give an explanation for the window controls which can be available in any GNOME utility window. The Ubuntu parents have long past through a whole lot of attempt to create an appealing, catchy background, set of fonts, window decorations, and manipulate buttons for any applications that you begin on your Ubuntu system

Figure 5.1

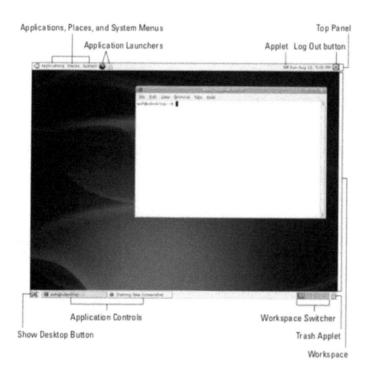

- Top Panel: A panel is a special portion of your computing device, controlled via the gnome panel application, which gives access to various methods of interacting with the laptop and launching different kinds of packages. GNOME can display panels along any fringe of the screen, but the default GNOME configuration shows panels on the pinnacle and backside of the display screen. Via default, the top panel incorporates the following items:

- Places, Applications, and system Menus: A menu includes a list of shortcuts to specific commands, tasks, or packages. These three menus provide clean, graphical access to applications, portions of your pc system or community locations, and system associated duties, respectively. Every of these menus is described in greater element inside the next segment, "Menus in GNOME." To display any of these panel menus, you simply left click at the call of the menu, and the associated menu drops down and shows in your display. To shut the menu, virtually left click on someplace else on the screen.
- Application Launchers: those icons start particular packages for you while you left click on them.
- Applets: those icons release lightweight applications that run in the context of a panel and offer numerous abilities. Including and configuring applets is discussed later on this chapter within the section entitled "Customizing Panels."
- Log out Button: This button quickly terminates your current login session and representations the GNOME login supervisor.

- N Workspace: this is the portion of the display in which packages execute and show associated home windows and dialogs.

- N backside Panel: This panel is displayed at the bottom of the display screen and incorporates the subsequent items by default:

  - Show desktop Button: This button minimizes all windows and dialogs that are currently displayed on the display, revealing the current computer.
  - Application Controls: every software that is lively to your current workspace presentations an associated manage place on this portion of the lowest panel. Right clicking in this control minimizes and maximizes the software, whilst left clicking on this manage displays a context touch menu for moving and controlling that software's window(s).
  - Workspace Switcher: this is a special applet that enables you to manage a couple of workspaces and gives a miniature display of every energetic workspace. Workspaces are essentially separate digital monitors that are furnished by way of the GNOME desktop. You could run packages on different workspaces, pass applications between workspaces, and so on. A couple of workspaces offer a convenient manner of running distinctive styles of programs on distinct digital monitors without them being seen till you really switch to the workspace in which they are displayed. A common instance of whilst this is useful is when you're at work and need to play a sport you can start the sport on an extraordinary workspace from the only in which you're truly operating, and

switch to it every time nobody is asking over your shoulder.

- Trash Applet: this is a special applet that gives get access to the Trash Can, that's a unique part of the GNOME computing device to which you could drag files to ultimately delete them.

241

Chapter 6

6.1 Command line tools

Due to the fact Linux has its conceptual roots in the older Unix operating device, many Linux programs are designed to be carried out from a command line. A command line is the conventional interface found on older laptop systems that may not have used the hard decision, graphically oriented monitors that most of the people expect nowadays. Inside the command line version, the device runs an application, referred to as a command line interpreter, which does just what its call indicates. A command line interpreter reads the instructions which you type, locates the suitable software in your device, and executes that utility for you as informed based on what you've typed. As soon as the command completes, the command interpreter presentations a sequence of characters, referred to as a spark off, signifying that it is ready to accept any other command.

6.2 Executing Commands

The ls command lists information about files and directories for your Ubuntu device. The Linux ls command is an updated version of a traditional Unix application by using the same name. In authentic Unix style, nobody became inclined to kind extra characters like "i" and "t", so the command was given the quick to kind abbreviation of ls. Whilst utilized by itself on the command line, the ls command truly shows the contents of the modern listing, as within the following example:

```
$ ls
```

exec_commands.txt   hey.c   hey.o
include_example.c

Include_testexample

Hey   hey.foo   hey.s
include_example.out

You could additionally deliver the name of a specific report or listing as an argument to the ls command, as within the following examples:

```
$ ls hey
```

Hey

Using the ls command to list the call of a file that you already know is spectacularly uninteresting (even though it can be very useful while mixed with wildcards, which might be). However, listing a directory suggests the contents of that directory, as in the following instance:

```
$ ls include_testexample
```

Libxml2 net_dev system

The output from this command indicates that the include_testexample listing itself carries three other documents or directories. I befell to recognize that include_testexample become a listing if you're now not certain what styles of matters are in the modern listing, you can use the ls command's F option to provide you with this data. For example, here's the edge directory as shown the use of the ls F command:

```
$ ls  F
```

Boot_services.txt hey.c   hey.o include_example.c

Include_testexample/

Hey*   hey.foo hey.s include_example.out

The ls command's F option decorates the names of the items in the current directory with an extra character to perceive any item that isn't in reality a text report. An asterisk following the call of an object indicates that this is an executable document, at the same time as a reduce ("/") following the call of an item indicates that this is certainly a directory. The ls command's F alternative may be very useful, but (in genuine Linux fashion) isn't the most effective manner to get certain statistics approximately each of the items in the current directory. You can also get this type of data the usage of different options to the ls command. For instance, one of the maximum normally used alternatives to the ls com mand is the l option, which means that "display output in long format." The use of this option offers a variety of additional statistics about the objects within the modern listing, as inside the following instance:

$ ls l

Total 40

-rw-r-r—1   health   users   783   2021.0705   12:15 boot_services.txt

-rwxr-xr-x   1 health users 924 2021.0705 12:16 hey

-rw-r-r—1 health users 61 2021.0705 12:17 hey.c

-rw-r-r—1 health users 61 2021.0705 12:17 hey.foo

-rw-r-r—1 health users 2501 2021.0705 12:17 hey.o

-rw-r-r—1 health users 855 2021.0705 12:17 hey.s

-rw-r-r—1   health   users   201   2021.0705   12:17 include_example.c

-rw-r-r—1   health   users   733   2021.0705   12:17 include_example.out

-drwxr-xr-x 5health users 4091 2021.0705 12:17 include_testexample

As you could see, the lengthy option shows greater whole information about the documents and directories inside the cur hire directory. From left to right, this facts includes the subsequent: present day permissions, the range of difficult hyperlinks to that document inside the Linux filesystem (greater about that later in this segment), the owner and group, size, the date and time at which it turned into remaining modified, and the record or listing name.

As mentioned formerly, you could integrate alternatives and arguments on the equal command line to refine the conduct of maximum command line utilities. For instance, to get a protracted list of the contents of the include_testexample   listing,   you'll   execute   the subsequent command:

$ ls l include_test

Total 0

Drwxr-xr-x   2 health customers 70 2021.0705 12:17 libxml2

Drwxr-xr-x   2   health   customers   81   2021.0705 12:17 net_dev

Drwxr-xr-x   4   health   users   94   2021.0705   12:17 system

One more very popular option to the ls command is an option, which suggests all of the objects within the contemporary directory. By default, the ls command doesn't display items whose names begin with a period (aka full prevent). This is because all Linux directories include two unique entries that many humans don't care approximately, however which might be useful to traverse and aid the hierarchical structure of a Linux filesystem. These are the "." Access, which usually refers to the modern listing, and the ".." Entry, which constantly refers back to the parent of the current directory. The usage of the ls a command to examine the contents of the modern directory shows the following:

$ ls a

.   Hey.c
include_example.c   .can_run_me_now

..   Hey.foo include_example.out

Boot_services.txt hey.o   include_testexample

Hey   hey.s   .my_todo_directory

You'll note that the "." And ".." Entries are indexed inside the first column. But you'll additionally word that two new files have seemed inside the listing. Those are the files .my_todo_directory and .can_run_me_now, that are indexed inside the directory listing primarily based on the primary alphanumeric individual of their names due to the fact the ls command ignores leading durations whilst sorting document names (except, of course, the filename has no other characters as is the case with the ". " and ".. " entries, which therefore seem first inside the listing).

6.3 Shell

A shell is the general name given to any Linux command line interpreter, and is derived from Unix, the conceptual determine of Linux. Unix was one of the first running structures to introduce the concept of the usage of a command line interpreter that was now not constructed into the working system and which had no unique permissions to do mysterious working system responsibilities. These ideas were preserved in each conceptual descendant of Unix and feature proved available for several motives. The maximum thrilling of those is that, due to the fact it's far a separate, stand on my own executable, a Linux system can provide each consumer their option of a couple of shells, all of which can be upgraded independently from the working system.

6.4 Getting to Shell

Figure 6.1

The GNOME Terminal application

Figure 6.2

Multiple tabs in the GNOME Terminal

251

Chapter 7

7.1 Text Files on Ubuntu

Most of us people are used to operating with files in numerous application specific codecs, regularly recognized by way of their file extension or a special icon in your graphical computing device. We're all acquainted with the document files produced by way of graphical word processors inclusive of Microsoft word, pdf files utilized by Adobe Acrobat and other PDF readers, xls files produced by means of spreadsheets together with Excel, fm files produced through FrameMaker, ppt documents produced with the aid of PowerPoint, and so on. All of these documents comprise application records in a particular, frequently binary, format that lets the associated application make the best viable use of those documents, but which regularly makes them tough to use with any application apart from the only that created them.

7.2 Using vi

Vi is a modal editor (which, in case you skipped the previous phase, method that the same keys do different things depending on the mode that you're in). The primary vi modes are the following:

- Normal: vi is in everyday mode whilst you first start vi. In this mode you may enter all of the standard cursor movement and textual content deletion commands, but no longer input textual content into the file which you are enhancing. This is the number one source of confusion for brand spanking new vi customers, because most people anticipate to begin an editor and begin modifying text.
- Insert: in this mode, typing the same old alphanumeric and image keys on your keyboard enters the ones characters into the document which you are enhancing. Insert mode Is the mode that the general public count on to be in while you begin a text editor. The fact that after in insert mode, you want to press a special key (the escape key) to go back to command mode, is the second primary source of confusion for brand new vi users who locate themselves trapped in insert mode.
- Command line: in this mode, the cursor is positioned at the lowest line of your vi window, and you can enter a single line that is interpreted as a vi command, seek request, or a request to invoke an external command on a part of the report that you are enhancing (frequently called a filter command).

7.3 Inserting text in vi

When you've commenced vi, you'll without a doubt need to start developing the program, letter, or different record that you're operating on. As cited inside the preceding section, starting vi leaves you in regular mode, wherein you could pass the cursor and input commands, however not clearly input text. To start inserting text, kind the i command. This causes vi to enter insert mode. Any characters which you type might be inserted into the document that you are enhancing until you go out from insert mode. As a reminder, the very best manner to exit from insert mode is by urgent the getaway key to your keyboard. The use of the command starts off evolved putting textual content at the current cursor role, which can be awkward. In case you need to start including textual content without delay after the current cursor position, use a command. To start appending textual content after the end of the current line, use the A command. The a and A are just specialized commands for entering insert mode at a particular point to go out insert mode after the usage of these instructions, press the escape key.

7.4 Emacs Terminology

Due to the fact GNU emacs is designed to engage with a graphical window supervisor, need to use slightly different terminology to describe what you see at the screen. Figure 7.1 suggests windows on an Ubuntu device, each running emacs however travelling special files. Each emacs window has its very own menu bar and toolbar. The window within the foreground shows distinct files, each in its very own buffer. Every emacs buffer has a mode line at the bottom, which presents statistics about the file being considered in that buffer and its country. At the bottom of every emacs window is a standing line in that you interact with emacs, or wherein emacs shows any messages displayed via a selected emacs function.

Figure 7.1

Chapter 8

8.1 Creating and Publishing Documents

This chapter explains the way to do various types of phrase processing in your Ubuntu Linux gadget. It starts through discussing the various markup languages, which can be textual content format ways of making formatted documents in a text editor for your Ubuntu Linux system. Even though really antique school, markup languages are still famous, and Ubuntu supports famous, open source, markup-oriented document production structures consisting of tex, and even a similar to the venerable system from bygone Unix days.

8.2 Document Markup Language on Ubuntu

Long, when people just used terminals, word processing supposed developing documents in a textual content editor and embedding unique commands to inform a few other software the way to layout your file for a particular target printer. The layout wherein these documents had been created is referred to as a markup language, of which the most common example is HTML. Of route, HTML is designed to markup documents which are centered for use as internet pages, but the same concepts apply. Growing files in markup languages is still popular in educational and publishing circles due to the fact many institutions and journals use textual content documents in a markup language as the lowest commonplace denominator for submissions. This allows them to combine documents from a couple of sources into a single, stylistically constant book without disturbing about what model of word every person used, what fonts they'd used, and so on. Tex (reported tech) is a typesetting application and related markup language that is designed to produce extraordinarily fantastic output, mainly for clinical and mathematical notation. Eminent computer scientist Donald Knuth wrote tex in 1977, largely because he needed a definitely incredible device for producing the three volumes of his "artwork of pc Programming" series. If it wasn't cool sufficient to jot down your own report formatting machine, Knuth firstly wrote tex in a machine of his personal called internet, which is a combination of documentation and Pascal source code in a single supply report. The supply code is extracted from the internet record the use of a software called tangle, and the formatted supply code and included documentation is extracted (in tex format, of path) using a software called weave. None of which topics in case you simply want to apply tex, however it's far pretty pleasing and feels like a recursive episode of "laptop Scientists long gone Wild" (available soon on DVD), so I notion which you would possibly revel in including this tidbit in your series of exciting but nonessential knowledge.

Many different implementations of tex are available nowadays, all extracted from the unique tex.net document, converted into different languages, and a few more suitable to add extra capabilities. The supply code for tex is freely available, but so as for anything primarily based on the tex source code to name itself tex, it need to skip a tex formatting torture take a look at called experience. The version of tex provided within the Ubuntu repository (as on most Linux systems in recent times) is tetex, a complete tex distribution for Unix like structures this is essential tainted via Thomas Esser (for this reason the "te" in tetex).

8.3 Information regarding tex and Latex

Due to the fact tex and latex had been used for many years on a wide form of structures, a wonderful quantity of data about using them is available on the net. A simple net seek will turn up greater hits than you can in all likelihood need. As a timesaver, a number of my favored sites for data approximately tex and latex are the subsequent:

- Attending to grips with latex (www.andyroberts.net/misc/latex/index.html) is a terrific series of tutorials on the usage of latex from Andrew Roberts.
- Introduction to latex (www.math.uiuc.edu/~hildebr/tex/path) is a quick direction prepared at the university of Illinois department of mathematics, and offers a pleasant, short review of tex and latex.
- Text Processing with latex (www.eng.cam.ac.united kingdom/assist/tpl/textprocessing) is an outstanding website online at the college of Cambridge in the United Kingdom that provides many online tutorials and examples of making a variety of files using latex.

- The tetex HOWTO
(www.tldp.org/HOWTO/tetexhowto.html) was
written a few years ago, but one of the nice things
approximately solid software program like tex and
latex is that things don't exchange an awful lot. This
file offers a bargain of general statistics about
creating tex and latex files, in addition to unique
information about the use of the tetex tex
implementation provided on your Ubuntu Linux
system.

Several books dedicated to tex and latex are available,
no discussion of tex and latex would be entire without
identifying the two seminal texts for each of those:

- Textbook with the aid of Donald E. Knuth
(Addison Wesley expert, 1984, ISBN:
0201134489)
- Latex: A file preparation system, 2d
version through Leslie Lamport (Addison Wesley
Expert, 1994, ISBN: 0201529831)

Given that those books are by the authors of the
respective structures, you could surely recollect them to
be definitive. Some modifications have honestly been
made to latex given that its introduction by means of
Lamport long in the past, however those are still the
seminal bibles of both document training systems.

8.4 Installation of files for writer

Writer is set up by means of default in case you deploy Ubuntu from the live CD, from the change set up CD the usage of the textual content Mode installer, and from the change installer the usage of the OEM Mode installer. If you need to feature creator or the whole openoffice.org suite to a server device that has a graphical consumer interface, you can deploy them using apt get, flair, or Synaptic, as explained in bankruptcy 20, "adding, doing away with, and Updating software."

One of the matters that differentiates Ubuntu Linux from different Linux distributions is its intense dedication to the consumer, specifically in terms of internationalization. If you are best running in a single language, the correct localization applications to your physical location are set up together with your default Ubuntu set up. However, in case you are putting in writer to be used while creating files in more than one languages, you can additionally need to search for and deploy the best hyphenation, localization, and glossary applications for anything different locales you are writing for. You may effortlessly find those by looking for a string that represents the united states code which you are seeking out. For instance, figure 8.1 suggests the specific German language help programs for openoffice.org that have been identified through trying to find the string "de" inside the Synaptic bundle supervisor.

Figure 8.1

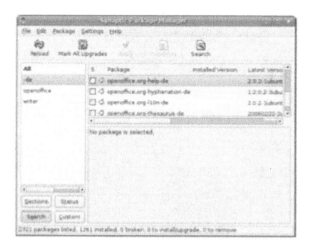

Personalizing Writer

The first aspect that you'll want to do whilst getting started with creator is to go into a few information about yourself into its consumer data fields. That is generally beneficial due to the fact writer will use this records in numerous locations while filling out fields in documents that you create the usage of the openoffice.org Wizards (as explained within the next phase).

Choose the equipment ⇨ options menu object to show the options conversation's consumer records shape, as shown in figure 8.2. Fill out the fields on this form and click on adequate to go back to author and your file.

Figure 8.2

Conclusion

Linux is an opensource working system like windows and MacOS. It isn't always just constrained to the running machine, but these days, it's also used as a platform to run computer systems, servers, and embedded systems. It gives various distributions and versions as it is open source and has a modular design. The kernel is a middle a part of the Linux system. Linux system is used to manipulate numerous offerings inclusive of system scheduling, software scheduling, fundamental peripheral gadgets, record device, and extra. Linux gives diverse blessings over different operating systems such as home windows and macOS. So, it is used in nearly each subject, from cars to home equipment and smartphones to servers (supercomputers). This book has provided you the complete guide and rich information regarding Linux. Absorbing all the components described and using it will open up you to the new world of Linux.

CPSIA information can be obtained
at www.ICGtesting.com
Printed in the USA
LVHW020028250521
688313LV00018B/1584

9 781802 264067